# Towards Understanding

# Islam...

و

By

# Abul A'la Maududi

Revised and edited by Yahiya Emerick

ISBN: 1450552013
EAN-13: 9781450552011

# Table of Contents

# Towards Understanding Islam

# 1
# What is Islam?

In almost every case, the religions of our world are usually named after either the people who founded them or by the culture or country from which they sprang. Christianity, for example, gets its name from Jesus Christ. Buddhism comes from the Buddha, Zoroastrianism from Zoroaster, and Judaism, the ancient faith of the Jewish people, takes its name from both the tribe of Judah and the land of Judea from whence it originated. Other more localized religions, and even the various sub-sects of the major faiths, also follow a similar pattern. Islam, however, breaks with this pattern. It is the only world faith whose very name has no relationship to any person or culture.

The name Islam doesn't fit the usual practice of name/place identification for the very reason that it's not a faith that can be claimed by any one person, culture or nation. It wasn't something created by any man to serve the needs of his local people at a particular time and place. It's a universal faith, open to all humanity, whose primary goal is to cultivate within each and every one of us the reality of submission to God, i.e. Islam.

So Islam, as you can now see, is a descriptive name. Anyone who possesses the substance of what this name implies, regardless of their race, culture, nation or ancestry, is a Muslim. (The words Islam and Muslim are related, as you will soon see.) It is from the Muslim holy book, the Qur'an that we learn that all throughout human history, and in all places, there have been good and righteous people who fit the very definition of a Muslim, even if they didn't call themselves by that particular name. This then begs the question: What does Islam really mean, and how can righteous people from all across the ages, who seemingly had no contact with it, be called Muslims?

## What Does Islam Really Mean?

Islam is an Arabic word that means to submit, to surrender, to be obedient to something and also to be at peace. Given that the Islamic faith calls for complete submission and obedience to God, it is easy to see why the very religion itself is labeled, Islam.

---

**Islam**= Submission to God
**Muslim**= A person who submits to God

---

All of us can see that we live in a well-ordered universe. There are natural laws and precisely defined principles that can be discovered in every part of nature in our vast cosmos. Everything seems to have its place in a great plan, if you will, and functions perfectly. The sun, the moon, the stars, and all the other celestial bodies are knit together in such a wonderfully synchronized system that one is literally awe-struck at their magnificence. All of these heavenly bodies adhere to unalterable laws of physics and don't deviate even for an instant from their exact trajectories. The earth rotates on its axis, and in its orbit around the sun it never fails to follow the same, reliable course. Everything in our universe, from the smallest spinning electron to the mightiest galaxies themselves constantly and ceaselessly follows their own physical laws. Matter, energy and even life itself all obey laws, or principles that govern their growth and transformation, as well as their life and also their death.

Even in the realm of human life, the laws of nature are obvious to see. A person's birth, growth and life are all regulated by a determined set of biological laws. Human beings derive nourishment from their environment through methods that don't change. All the organs of the body, from the smallest cells, on up to the heart and brain, function according to the operating guidelines set out for them. All of this evidence points to the fact that we have a universe that is governed by law, and that everything within it adheres to the course that the laws of nature have set for it.

The source for this system of galactic law, as irresistible and unavoidable as it is, which governs everything that exists from the tiniest particles of matter to the most spectacular galaxies in the cosmos, is the Law of God, the Creator and Ruler of the Universe. Now, because all created things obey the Law of God, the entire universe, is, by extension, following the way of Islam, for Islam literally means nothing less than complete obedience and submission to God, the Caretaker of the Universe. By extension, the sun, the moon, the earth and all other celestial bodies can then be termed, Muslims, i.e. submitted ones. Even the very air we breathe, itself, along with the water and soil of our world are Muslims. This term can be expanded to living creatures as well, such as the insects, birds, fish and mammals of our living world and even to the plants, trees, vegetables and fruits. Everything in the universe, both living and non-living, is Muslim, in that they all obey Almighty God by submitting to His structure of natural Law.

Even a person who denies that God exists, or who believes in something other than the One God, is obligated to be a Muslim in as much as his bodily functions are concerned. That is because his entire biological life, from his earliest stirrings in the womb until his body turns to dust after death, is governed by the principles of God's Law. His every molecule, tissue and limb must endlessly obey the universal laws laid down for them by Almighty God. His tongue, which in his ignorance may actively deny God, or which says that there are many gods, is by its very physical nature a Muslim.

His head, which he may willingly bow to another besides God, is Muslim. His heart, with which he ignorantly loves others besides his Creator, is also intuitively Muslim. Indeed, all of these physical parts of the body are obedient to Divine Law, and their functions and biological operations are governed by the dictates of that Law alone. This is the basic position of both human beings and the wider universe, i.e. all are submitted to God's Laws, and therefore all are Muslims. Now let's look at the issue from a different perspective.

In every human being's life there are two separate aspects of existence. In other words, there are two separate spheres to his life that are operating at the same time. On the one hand he finds himself completely dependent on the divinely directed natural world. He can't escape from it or redirect it. Nor can he ever slip away from its irresistible control over him. For instance, no one has control over the power of nature all around them.

Natural disasters occur and we can't escape them, or limit their destructiveness. In some regions of the earth, hurricanes and tropical storms rage. Other regions suffer from extreme cold and blizzards, or even tornadoes, earthquakes and volcanic eruptions. No one is safe from these kinds of overwhelming disasters. And it's during these times that people may call upon that very God Who can control these processes, Whose help they never bothered to seek (until disaster struck).

There is another sphere to our lives as well. Since we have been blessed with reason and intelligence we have the power to think and to make judgments, to choose or to deny, to adopt or to spurn. We have the freedom to follow whatever way of life we choose. We can select any religion, join any lifestyle, and fashion our lives according to whatever principles we like. What's more, we can even make up our own rules or blindly accept someone else's. So while we may have little control over what happens around us, we have been given a measure of free will and can chalk out our course of conduct within this world. In this way, we, unlike any other creature, have been blessed with freedom of choice, thought and action. Both of these different, contrary spheres of our life are real, co-existing, and yet are easily separated from each other upon examination.

In the first sphere, like all other creatures, human beings are born Muslim, for they are constantly obeying the orders of Almighty God (in their biological functioning and helplessness in the face of nature) and are bound to do so. As for the second sphere of their lives, (the ability to choose what to believe in and to act accordingly,) people are free to become or not to become a conscious Muslim. It's that freedom of choice, and how it is exercised, that divides all humanity into one of two groups: the believers in God, and those who disbelieve in God.

An individual who chooses to recognize the Creator, and accepts Him as his real Master, who honestly and faithfully submits to His Laws and follows the way of life He has revealed for all humanity, thereby becomes a whole Muslim. Such a person has achieved completeness in his Islam (submission to God) by consciously deciding to obey God through the use of those very abilities of free thought, choice and action which God Almighty blessed him with. Now his entire

14

life will become characterized by obedience to God. There is no longer any conflict between the physical aspect of his nature and his inner feelings for now he will redirect himself to spend both his time and energy seeking the pleasure of his Creator. He is a perfect Muslim and his Islam is complete. The submission of his entire self to the will of God is Islam and nothing but Islam.

He will now consciously submit to the One Whom he was already obeying (biologically) without even realizing it. He will now willingly offer obedience to the Master to Whom he had already given obedience to unintentionally. His knowledge of the truth of all things will now be more complete, for he will finally acknowledge the One Who blessed him with the ability to learn and to know.

From this point forward, his reasoning and judgment will be set on an even plane, for he will have correctly decided to obey the One Who was responsible for giving him the faculties of thought and judgment. Even his tongue will now be in a natural state, for it will truthfully declare that it was the Lord Most High Who endowed it with the gift of speech.

His entire existence will now be an example of wholeness as he both voluntarily and involuntarily obeys the laws of the One God, the Master of the Universe. Throughout his life he will serve the Being that the rest of the universe serves. This is the most natural way to live. Such an individual is truly God's representative on earth. The entire world is for him and he is for God.

## What does it mean to Deny God?

In contrast to the one who accepts God willingly (and thereby becomes whole in both their body and mind) there is another type of person. Although he came into this world ready to submit to God, he never used his skills of reason, intelligence and intuition to recognize his Lord and Creator. Rather, as he grew into maturity, he misused his freedom of choice by choosing to deny Him (or at least failing to recognize Him). Such an individual, by rejecting God, becomes a concealer of the truth that is plainly visible before his very own heart and eyes.

The operative Arabic word (that is often mistranslated as disbelief,) is *kufr*. It literally means to cover, to conceal or to suppress. The person who rejects God is called a concealer (*kafir*) because he conceals, through his disbelief, what is inherently in his own nature and fused into his soul. His natural biology is literally filled with Islam. His whole body, every cell, every atom, functions in obedience to that primary instinct.

Indeed, each and every particle that exists, whether alive or not, functions in accordance with Islam and is fulfilling the duty that has been assigned to it. But this person's vision has been blurred, his common sense has become fogged and he is literally unable to see the obvious. His own true nature has become hidden from his eyes, and he thinks and acts in complete disregard of it. Knowledge of the real truth has become separated from him and he gropes along blindly in the dark. This is what *kufr*, is like.

Concealment (*kufr*) is not just a form of ignorance; it is ignorance, pure and simple. What greater ignorance could there be than ignorance of God, the Creator and Caretaker of the Universe? When we view the vast panorama of nature, the greatest of all organic machines, and the grand design that exists in every nook and cranny of creation, the question has to be asked: "How can someone observe the grandness of all of this and not know who its Maker and Director is?" Such a person can even look into his own body and see how wonderful a system it is: it operates in a logical and intelligible fashion and helps him to achieve whatever goal he wishes.

Yet he is unable to understand the Force that brought him into existence, or the Engineer Who designed and produced that wonderful machine of his, or the Creator Who made this unique creature out of lifeless matter: carbon, calcium, sodium and so on. He sees the impressive plan through which the universe operates, but fails to see the Planner behind it. He sees beauty and harmony in its functioning, but not the Creator Who allows it to work. He observes that, yes, there is a definite design to nature, but he is completely blind to the Designer!

No matter which way he turns, he sees magnificent examples of skill in science and wisdom, math and engineering, design and purpose. Yet he ignores the Being Who brought into existence everything that inhabits this endless universe. How can someone who has blinded himself to this realization ever hope to come close to accurate knowledge of anything? How can the doors of ultimate truth and knowledge be open to him? Has anyone who started out in the wrong place ever reached the right destination? He will fail every time to find the clues that lead him to what is truly real.

The right path will remain hidden from him, and no matter how much he may excel in the sciences or in the arts, he will never be able to discover the light of truth and wisdom. He will always be groping in the darkness and stumbling in the gloom of ignorance. But that's not the worst of it. Concealment is also a form of oppression -the worst form that it can take! How do we define oppression in this instance? It's the cruel and unjust use of any force or power. If you force someone or something to act unjustly, or to act against its own true nature, will and natural inclination, then that is oppression, plain and simple.

We've already seen that everything in the universe is obedient to God, the Almighty Creator of everything that the world contains. To obey God and live according to His Will and Law, or to put it more precisely, to be a Muslim, is ingrained in the nature of all things. God has given human beings power over objects in the natural world, but it is superimposed upon their nature that their purpose is to fulfill the Will and Law of God and not otherwise.

The one who disobeys God and brings concealment of the truth into their hearts perpetrates the greatest injustice. He uses all of the God-given abilities of the body and mind to rebel against his natural state and becomes an unwitting instrument in the drama of disobedience. He forces his head to bow before gods other than the one true God. He cherishes in his heart the love, reverence and fear of other, lesser powers, and utterly disregards the instinctive urges of his own mind.

He uses his own power, and the power of all those things that he controls, to oppose the natural order of things, as expressed by the Will of God. In this way he establishes a reign of oppression. Can there be a greater example of injustice, tyranny and cruelty than the one exhibited by this person, who exploits and misuses everything under the sun, and forces them to follow a course that is against nature and right?

Concealment of the truth is not only oppression. It is, at the very least, sheer rebellion, ingratitude and treachery. After all, what is the real nature of a human being? What kind of power and authority does he have? Is he the creator of his own mind, heart and soul, or have they been created by God? Did he create the universe and everything in it, or was it created by God? Who created countless powers and energies like oil, electricity, solar power and atomic forces and made them fit for the service of humanity, human beings or God?

If everything was made by God and God alone, then to whom does everything really belong? Who is the real owner? Who is rightfully in charge of them? Clearly God is -and no one else. And if God is the Creator, the Master and the Sovereign, then who could be a greater rebel than the one who uses God's creation without following His rules, who bends his own mind to plot against God, who harbors in his soul thoughts against Him, and who uses his various abilities against the will of the Almighty?

If a servant betrays his master, you denounce him as untrustworthy. If a soldier betrays his own country, you call him a traitor and a renegade. If a person cheats his friend, you don't hesitate to call him ungrateful. But what can compare to the level of this ultimate betrayal, this ingratitude and rebellion that the concealer of truth commits by his denial of God, the source of all power and authority?

Who gave humanity their control over the natural resources all around them? Who elevates people to positions of authority and power? Who gives presidents, kings and governors their power to rule, and who is the true provider and distributor of wealth? Whatever people possess and any good which they use to help others are gifts from God. The greatest social obligation that people have is to their parents, but who implanted in the parents' hearts the desire to love and nurture their children? Who gave the mother the will and the power to care for and nourish her children?

A moment of reflection will reveal that God is the greatest caretaker of humanity. He is the Creator, Master, Nourisher, Sustainer, and our real Ruler. If this is the actual position of God with regards to humanity, what greater betrayal, ingratitude, rebellion and treason can there be other than *kufr*. Concealment of the truth is the means by which an individual denies and disobeys his real Master and Ruler.

A 16th century model of the solar system. Early Muslim scientists, acting upon the advice of the Qur'an, used their energies to observe and chart the celestial bodies in order to better appreciate the creation of God and the lessons it can teach.

Is it possible for people to do any harm to God, through their disobedience and denial? Not in the least. Humanity is an insignificant speck on the face of a tiny sphere within this limitless universe. What harm can people do to the Master of the Universe, whose property is so infinitely vast that we cannot even come close to exploring its boundaries, even with the most powerful telescopes or fastest spacecraft?

What harm can any one do to God, Whose power is so vast that innumerable celestial bodies like the earth, moon, sun and stars are at His command, whirling about like tiny marbles? His wealth is so boundless that He is the sole Master and Controller of the entire universe. He provides for all and doesn't need anything from anyone. Humanity's revolt against Him can't harm Him in the least. On the contrary, by their disobedience, people are treading a path that will lead them to total ruin and disgrace.

The inevitable result will be a failure to achieve the most basic, and most important, purpose of life, a purpose that was ordained by God for humanity. Rebels against God will not find the path to true knowledge and vision. They will never find its secrets for they have denied the existence of the One Who created it. Their intelligence and reason will always go astray, because reason which fails to recognize the Being Who created it cannot illumine the pathways of life. Without this clear light brightening its way, humanity can never recognize and put these truths into practice in daily life.

The result is that people like this will meet failure in every undertaking they embark upon. Their moral, civil and social lives will be in disarray, while their struggles for prosperity and family success will fall short, in other words, their whole lives will be in turmoil. Disorder and confusion will emanate from them all over the world. They will, without hesitation, shed blood, violate the rights of others, be cruel to them and oppress them. Through their behavior they will breed disorder and destruction in the world. Their perverted minds, blurred vision, distorted values and self-perpetuating vices will make life miserable both for themselves and those around them.

These are the people who will destroy the peace and tranquility of life on earth. Tyranny, arrogance, destruction and mayhem will be sure to follow. In the afterlife, they will be held accountable for the crimes they committed against their own natures, skills and inner inclinations. Every organ of their body- their brains, eyes, hands and feet- will complain against the injustice and cruelty they were forced to participate in. Every cell of their body will berate them before God Who, as the source of all justice, will give them the full punishment they deserve. This is the humiliating consequence of concealing the truth. It leads to the dead end of total failure, both in this life and in the afterlife.

23

# Where Does Islam Fit In?

Now that we have discussed the drawbacks and pitfalls of concealing the God-given truth that people should recognize, we shall now turn to Islam, as a living phenomenon, and examine the ways that it relates to life. In the wide world around you, as well as in your more immediate surroundings, you can find countless signs of God's Divine power. If we can recall for a moment this magnificent universe, which never ceases to operate with an uncanny sense of order of organization, we can see that if functions in harmony with natural laws that cannot be changed. This, in itself, is a witness to the fact that its Creator, Designer and Governor is a Supreme Being Who must have awareness and control over everything.

The awesome scope of this vast universe and all it contains is proof that this Being has command over unimaginable resources. He is the Most Powerful Being, perfectly wise, and nothing in this universe dares to go against His will. It is in the very nature of a human being, along with all other things in the universe, to obey Him. In fact, people are already obeying one aspect of His Law, namely in their biology, even if they don't realize it. The moment people try to go against this Law, by interfering with their bodies' normal requirements; they bring themselves perilously close to death and destruction. This is what we observe in nature everyday.

Besides giving human beings the ability to learn, think, ponder and distinguish between right and wrong, God granted us a certain amount of free-will and freedom of action. It is within this freedom that our test in this world lays. Our knowledge and intelligence, our ability to tell the good from the bad, and our freedoms of choice and action are constantly being tried and tested.

In this trial, no one is forced to follow a specific direction, for the purpose of the trial would be defeated by compulsion. If you're taking an exam, and then you find yourself forced to write down a specific answer to a question, the examination won't be of any use. Your proficiency can only be properly judged if you're allowed to answer the question freely and according to what you know about the subject at hand. If your answers are wrong, you fail, and that failure may hinder your future success and progress.

The situation that people face in this world is exactly the same. God has given us free will and freedom of action so that we can be free to choose whatever way of life we like and feel is for our benefit- Islam (submission to God) or *kufr* (concealing the truth of God from our eyes).

People can be classified into two general categories. On the one hand, there are those who neither understand their own nature, nor their place within the cosmos. They err in recognizing who their real Master is, and they fail to envision His qualities. They also tend to misuse their freedom and pursue paths of disobedience and revolt. These people have failed in their test and failed to properly employ their knowledge, intelligence and sense of personal responsibility. They've failed to rise to the standard for which they have been made and they don't deserve any better destiny than mediocrity.

On the flip side, another category of people are those who are successful in this life's test. They correctly used their knowledge and intelligence and thus recognized their Creator. They put their faith in Him and chose obedience to Him even though nobody forced them into it. They're better able to tell right from wrong, and they choose what is moral even though they may be tempted to sin. They understand their nature, realizing all its fundamentals and truths and adopt the way of loyalty and obedience to God, the Creator, even though they could have easily chosen some other way. They're successful in this trial because they have skillfully used their ability to think and to reason.

All of their faculties are now employed in the service of the truth. They open their eyes to reality. They use their ears to listen for the truth. They engage their minds in the search for correct knowledge, and they direct their hearts and souls towards following the right way that they've adopted. They chose the truth. They see the Reality, and willingly and joyfully submit to their Lord and Master. They're intelligent, truthful and dutiful, for they've chosen light over darkness. Indeed, it was after seeing this very light that they responded enthusiastically. Thus they've proven (by their own conduct) that they're not only seekers after truth, but that they've also recognized it and chosen to serve it as well. They're clearly on the right path and they're bound to succeed in this world and in the life to come.

These kinds of people will always choose the right path in every field of knowledge and human endeavor. The one who knows God by recognizing all of His attributes knows where the beginning and end of all reality lies. He can never be led astray, for his first step is on the right path. He is sure of his direction and the destination towards which his life is moving. When he thinks deeply, he'll concentrate on the mysteries of the universe and nature, but unlike many errant philosophers, he won't lose his way in a maze of doubt and skepticism. His path is illuminated with Divine Vision; every step he takes will lead him in the right direction.

When he engages in scientific inquiry, he will try to unravel the laws of nature, uncover the hidden treasures of the earth, and master all the unknown forces of the mind and of matter, all for the improvement of humanity. He will try his utmost to explore all avenues of knowledge and research, to harness all that exists in the earth as well as in space for the service of humanity. But at every stage of his search, his constant awareness of God's Reality will prevent him from using his scientific discoveries for wickedness or destruction.

He will never imagine himself, nor make the claim, that he is the master of the universe, boasting that he tamed nature. He will never make himself out to be a god of sorts and won't harbor ambitions of subverting the world for his devious plans. He won't try to enslave the human race or oppress people, nor will he attempt to gain ascendancy over everyone and everything, whether through fair or devious means. That kind of attitude of revolt and defiance against God and his orderly universe can never be found in a real Muslim scientist. Only a scientist inflicted with *kufr* can fall victim to such delusional visions. Such a person would expose the entire human race to the danger of total destruction and annihilation.

The Qur'an, the holy book of Islam, is often written in very fancy calligraphy to emphasize the beauty of its message, both when recited aloud and when read and studied. Here are the opening verses of chapter two of the Qur'an.

In contrast to this, a Muslim scientist will behave quite differently. The deeper his insight into the vast wonders of science, the stronger his faith in God will be. His head will readily bow down before Him in gratitude. He will carry the conviction that since his Master has blessed him with greater understanding and knowledge; he must live up to that trust and work diligently both for his own betterment and also for the advancement of all people. His own exercise of free-will won't lead him to promote violence or destruction. He'll be guided, instead, by the principles of morality and Divine Revelation. So rather than becoming an agent of mere destruction and chaos in our world, science, through his able hands, will become an instrument for the welfare of all humanity. In this manner, the scientist expresses his thankfulness to his Master for the many gifts and blessings that He has given to the human race.

Likewise, whether in the field of history, economics, politics, law or any of the other branches of the arts and sciences, a Muslim will not long lag behind someone who has concealed the truth of God's sovereignty from their own hearts. How the believer and the concealer view their professions, and the procedures they employ to gain knowledge in them, will differ widely. A Muslim will study every branch of knowledge, but will keep that knowledge in its proper perspective. He will work hard to realize his purpose in life and, through his study, will arrive at truly valid and whole conclusions.

The historian will learn from the past experiences of humanity, and will discover the root causes for the rise and fall of civilizations. He will try to absorb the lessons that made previous nations successful, as well as be wary of what made them decline and disappear. The politician will strive with all his heart and soul for the establishment of a government where peace, brotherhood, equality and goodness reign.

He will work for a system of government that promotes the proposition that every human being is as a brother to his fellows, where exploitation and slavery are banned, and where the rights of the individual are respectfully upheld. He will desire to participate in the making of just such a government in which the powers of the state are considered a sacred trust from God and are used for the common welfare of all.

In the field of law, the Muslim will seek to promote the application of real justice and he will prove to be an ardent protector of the rights of all- particularly of the powerless and marginalized. He will ensure that everyone gets their due share and that no injustice or oppression is inflicted upon anyone. He will respect the law, make others respect it, and will see that the law is administered justly and fairly.

The moral life of a sincere Muslim will always be characterized by godliness, goodness and honesty. He will pass his time in this world guided by the conviction that God, alone, is the Master of all things, that whatever material possessions he or others may possess are nothing more than gifts from God, and that any special talents he wields are a trust from that very same God.

He will assume that the freedom he has been endowed with is not something to be used up indiscriminately, and that his true interest lies in using it in agreement with God's Will. He will ever call to mind the realization that one day he will have to return to God Almighty and submit to an account of his entire life. Such a sense of accountability will remain so firmly embedded in his thoughts that he will automatically shun any and all irresponsible behavior.

> **"True wealth doesn't come from having an abundance of things. True wealth comes from having a contented mind."**
>
> -Prophet Muhammad, peace be upon him

Just think about the moral excellence of a person who lives within this mental framework: his life will be oriented towards purity, piety, love and altruism. He, himself, will be a blessing from God to the world! His mind won't be troubled with perverse thoughts or deranged ambitions. He will remove himself from even the possibility of seeing, hearing or doing what he knows to be sinful. He will guard his tongue and never speak any untruths. He will earn his living honestly and fairly and would rather go hungry than eat his dinner if it were gained through the wages of exploitation and injustice. He will never oppress people nor violate the sanctity of human life irrespective of race or color.

He will never yield to the forces of evil and corruption, regardless of what it may cost him. He will be an example of goodness and excellence and will stand out firmly for truth and justice even if it means giving up his life in the process. He will detest all forms of injustice and discrimination and will stand up for what is right, unfazed by any turmoil that may gather around him. Such a person will indeed be a force to be reckoned with! He is bound to succeed, for nothing on earth can discourage him or obstruct his way.

Due to his noble qualities and firmness, he will find himself honored and respected by others. His esteem will be immeasurable. How can humiliation ever overcome a person who will always refuse to lower his head, or open his palms for favors, to anyone other than God Almighty, the Master of the entire universe? Such a one will have more power and be more effective in his endeavors. His personal inner strength can never be eclipsed, for he fears no one save God and seeks blessings from no one other than Him. What force can ever possibly swerve him from the right path? What ill-suggestion can taint his conscience? What authority can debase his behavior?

He will be the wealthiest and richest of all, for who can be wealthier and more independent than the person who leads a life of simplicity, satisfaction and contentment? You won't find him being crass, indulgent nor greedy; rather you will see that he's satisfied with whatever he earns fairly and squarely. Even if heaps of ill-gotten gains are presented to him for the taking, he won't even look at them, let alone try to use them for his benefit. In his heart there is peace and contentment- who can have greater riches than that?

He will be respected, popular and loved. Who can be more admired than the one who lives a life of charity and kindness? He will be honest with everyone he meets and in every situation. He will carry out his duties sincerely and will promote the welfare of others earnestly. People's hearts will be naturally drawn to him, and they'll love and respect him for all of his good qualities.

He will be trusted by others and honored for his honesty. Who can be more reliable than someone like that, for he will never betray his trust, nor will he by lured away from the path of righteousness. He will be true in word and true in deed. Fairness and justice will be his primary concern in all affairs for he will be constantly aware that God is omni-present and sees all things. Words fail to describe the accolades and goodwill that such a person will command. Will there be anyone who distrusts him? Such is the life and character of a sincere Muslim.

If you understand the character of a true Muslim, you will be convinced that he can never long remain in a situation of humiliation, debasement or subjugation. He is certain to win in the end. No power on earth can overwhelm or subdue him, for Islam instills in him qualities that cannot be overshadowed by any passing fancy, vain pleasure or illusion.

After he has completed living his life of respectability and honor here on earth, the sincere Muslim will return to his Creator, Who will shower upon him the finest of His blessings. God will reward him because he discharged his duty as he should have, fulfilled his mission successfully and walked away from the test of life in triumph. He was successful in life and will thus be equally successful in the afterlife. He will live in eternal peace, joy and happiness.

This is Islam, the natural religion of human beings, the way of life that is not exclusively associated with any one person, ethnic group, time period or geographic location. In every age, in every nation, and among all people, there have always been godly people who have striven to live this very ideal. We say they were all Muslims, whether they knew the name Islam or not, for whatever name they called their religion, it signified Islam and nothing but Islam.

# 2
# Faith and Obedience

Islam means obedience to God. Common sense would dictate that this obedience cannot be fully realized unless we know something about the nature of life and have some conviction about the truths we uncover. What is it that we should know? What are the essentials which a person must understand in order to fashion his or her life in accordance with the Divine System? First of all, every individual should have as their goal to acquire an unshakable belief in the existence of God. Unless a person firmly believes that God is real, then how can he or she be obedient to Him?

Our faith teaches us that true knowledge of God begins with His attributes and qualities. Through knowing something about the nature of God, an individual can cultivate within him or herself the noblest of human traits and mold his or her life in virtue and godliness. If a person doesn't know that there is only One God, Who is the Creator, Ruler and Sustainer of the universe, and that there is no one else with any power save Him, then he may eventually fall prey to false gods, those man-made deities that were manufactured over many centuries all over the world. Such a deluded person might even begin to offer tribute to them and pray to them for favors. But if he knows that there is only one God, which in Islam is the most important attribute of all, then there is little chance of him falling victim to polytheism.

If a person knows that God sees, hears and knows everything that we do in public and in private- even our thoughts- then how can he afford to be defiant or disobedient to God? He will feel that he is constantly being observed and will behave well as a result. But a person who doesn't know (or accept) that God is one, unique and ever watchful, may unwittingly be mislead into disobedience to God.

The essential prerequisites that everyone must possess, if they want to pursue true submission to God, can only be developed by having accurate knowledge about God and Who He is. This knowledge of His basic nature and character is what helps purify a person's mind and soul, as well as his beliefs, morals and actions. Merely dabbling in this knowledge or trying to reduce it to academic arguments is no way to prepare for the task ahead. Every individual man or woman must have a strong conviction, rooted deep in their minds, so that they can be free from insidious doubts and misleading distortions.

Moreover, a person must know what the proper way to order their life is, for only by doing that can they begin to seek the pleasure of God. Unless we know what God approves and disapproves of, how can we choose wisely between the many alternatives that confront us each day? If we don't know anything about Divine Law, how can we follow it? So now we see that knowing God's Law and the way He wants us to order our lives is also extremely important. But here, again, just knowing is not enough. We must have full confidence and conviction that what we are learning about is, in fact, Divine in nature, and that our salvation lies in sticking to this code and no other. For knowledge without this conviction will fail to inspire a person to follow the right path, and he might still get lost in the blind alley of disobedience.

Lastly, each one of us must also know the consequences of belief and obedience and those of *kufr* and disobedience. We need to know what blessings will be showered upon us if we choose God's way and lead a life of purity, virtue, and obedience. We must also know what terrible and traumatic consequences will follow if we adopt the path of disobedience and revolt. It is knowledge of the afterlife that can help set us straight.

We must have an unwavering belief in the fact that death does not mean the end of life; that there will be a resurrection and that we will all be brought to the highest court of justice, to be presided over by God Himself; that on the Day of Judgment complete justice will prevail, and that good deeds will be rewarded and sinfulness punished. Everyone will get what they deserve and there will be no escape. This reality will come to pass. Having our sense of responsibility and accountability strengthened with this realization is essential for full compliance and obedience to the Law of God.

# Three Essential Doctrines

1. God is One. He is not male or female. He does not look like us. He has no children or spouse. He is not divided up into separate parts and He was never born into our world as a human. He can forgive without having to pay a price for our sin.

2. Life after Death. We are all endowed with a soul that will live again in an afterlife. Following a resurrection of the spirit in the future there is either eternal reward in heaven or damnation in Hell. Hell is not forever for everybody who will enter it. Some will get out after their term of punishment is reached and be admitted to heaven if they had at least some faith.

3. Day of Judgment. God will assemble all resurrected souls one day and show to each a complete record of their life, thoughts and actions. He will examine their faith, explain the truth of their intentions and will allow those who were wronged to get satisfaction. He will also forgive a great many sins as He wills. Our faith (or lack of it) will be proved, our deeds will be weighed on a scale and then heaven, Hell or a temporary mid-way point between the two will be our fate.

A person who knows nothing about the afterlife may think that the issue of obedience and disobedience is irrelevant. He may think that whether we listen to God or not we will all end up the same in the end, because after death all of us will rot away in our graves. While this may be true of our physical bodies, this attitude shows the height of disobedience in its rawest form: how can such a person ever acquiesce to all the inconveniences and tasks that are inextricably associated with the life of active obedience? How can they ever be expected to avoid sin and immorality when they feel that being good or bad won't bring anything positive or negative to their lives? With this kind of skewed attitude no one can acknowledge and submit to God's Law.

Nor can a person, who lacks a firm belief in the afterlife and in the Divine Court of Judgment, remain firm and steadfast in the turbulent waters of life, what with all its attraction to sin, crime and evil; for doubt and hesitancy can rob a person of his will to act contrary to his lusts. You can remain firm in your behavior only if you are firm in your beliefs. If you suffer from a wavering mind you cannot remain firm and resolute.

You can only follow a set course sincerely if you are absolutely sure of the benefits that will come to you by following it and of the losses and sorrow that will engulf you if you disobey it. Thus, a profound knowledge of the consequences of belief and *kufr* and of the afterlife (and how it relates to this life) is essential for directing our lives towards true obedience to God. These are the essential facts that we must be familiar with if we want to lead a life of sincere obedience to God, a way of life otherwise known as- Islam.

## What does it mean to Believe?

So far we have talked about faith in terms of knowledge and belief, but the word faith actually means something far deeper. In the Arabic language the word for faith means three things simultaneously: to believe, to be convinced of something and lastly, to feel secure. This unique word is *eman*. *Eman*, can be described as a firm belief, arising out of knowledge and conviction, which leads in turn to a feeling of security regarding one's own place in the vast scheme of things.

The first house of worship in Islam was built here in Quba, a small village just outside of Medina in Arabia, in the year 622. This is a modern structure that you see here.

The one who knows something about God, and then who places unshakable trust in His unitary nature, attributes, law, guidance, and in the Divine code of reward and punishment is called a believer. Having this kind of resolute faith leads us to live a life of obedience and submission to the will of God. Anyone who lives this life of submission to God is known as a Muslim.

As you may have guessed, without faith no one can be a Muslim. It is the indispensable element; the starting point without which no beginning can be made. The relationship of Islam to *eman* is the same as of a tree to its seed. Even as a tree can't grow tall and strong without first being a seed, in the same way it is not possible for a person, who has no belief to start with, to become a 'Muslim'.

Does this mean that everyone who calls him or herself a Muslim is automatically faithfully obedient to God? No, for just as it can happen that, in spite of planting the seed, the tree may not grow for any number of reasons, or if it sprouts, its growth may be impaired or impeded, in the same way, a person may have faith, but due to a number of weaknesses, he may not become a sincere and committed Muslim.

To review then what we have learned thus far, we find that faith is the starting point that leads each of us to embrace a life of submission to God, and that a person cannot become a Muslim without it. We have also learned that many can give lip service to Islam, but not everyone succeeds in imbibing it whole-heartedly. It really is quite possible that a person may have a glimmer of faith but, because of poor will power, inadequate instruction in their religion, or the influence of bad company, he or she may not be living the life of a truly devoted Muslim. To better understand the stark

41

differences between faith, disbelief and inconsistency, we can classify people into four general categories:

1. *Those who have firm faith. Their authentic faith makes them absolutely and sincerely submit to God. They follow the way of God and devote themselves heart and soul to seek His pleasure by doing what He likes and by avoiding what He dislikes. In their devotion to God they are even more passionate than an ordinary person is- who thinks about nothing else other than getting rich and famous. Such enthusiastic people who live only for God are true Muslims.*

2. *Those who have faith, who believe in God, His Law and the Day of Judgment, but whose faith is not deep and strong enough to make them totally submit to God. They are far below the rank of true Muslims and may deserve punishment for their laxity and misdeeds, but they are still counted as Muslims. They are backsliders and sinners but not rebels. They acknowledge the Sovereign and His Law and, although they are sometimes violating that very same Law, they have not revolted against the Sovereign. They admit His supremacy and their own guilt. Thus they are in the wrong and deserve some form of limited punishment, but Muslims they remain.*

3. *Those who don't possess any faith at all. These people refuse to acknowledge the sovereignty of God and are thus rebels against the Supreme Authority in the universe. Even if their behavior is not all that bad, and even if they aren't participating directly in vice and violence, they remain rebels and their apparent good deeds and charity are of little value. They're like outlaws. In the same way that doing a few good deeds doesn't suddenly make a career criminal reformed in the eyes of society, so too, the seeming good of those who*

*revolt against God cannot compensate for the magnitude of the wrong, revolt, and disobedience they represent.*

*4. Those who neither possess faith nor who do good deeds. They spread chaos in the world and perpetrate all kinds of violence and oppression. They are the worst of humanity for they are not only rebels against God's well-ordered universal code, but sinners and criminals as well.*

By clearly defining the various spiritual conditions of humanity, we can see that real success and salvation depends first on having faith in God. From this seed springs the ability to truly lead a life of obedience to God. The exact level of obedience practiced by any given individual may vary from perfect to substandard. But regardless, without at least a kernel of faith there can be no Islam. Where there is no faith there is no Islam. Where there is no Islam there are only people who conceal God's truth. Its form and extent may vary from person to person, but in the end it is still *kufr* and nothing but *kufr*. Faith, then, is the most important ingredient for living a life of true and total submission to God.

## How do We Learn about God?

Now the question arises: How do we learn Who God is so that we can come to believe in His attributes, His Law and in the Day when He will judge us all?

We have already referred to the countless proofs of God all around us in the natural world and in our own selves. Indeed, our very existence itself bears witness to the fact that there is a Creator and Governor over this great universe, and that He controls and directs it. These proofs in themselves reflect some of the Divine Attributes of the Creator: His wisdom, His extensive knowledge, His omnipotence, His mercy, His inexhaustible power, His varied ability-in short, evidence of His attributes can be found everywhere in His work.

But our intellect and capacity to acquire knowledge is sometimes flawed, through our own fault, in observing and understanding what it all really means. Indeed, signs of God's existence are all plain to see, and our eyes have the capacity to read what is written all over the face of creation, but people are often either indifferent or they miscalculate.

Some declare that there are two gods, one of good and one of evil, others begin to profess a belief in a three-in-one god, and still others succumbed to polytheism, or a belief in a god for everything. In this last category there are the nature-worshippers and the elemental worshippers, who believe in gods of rain, air, luck, death and more. So although the signs of a single, designing Mind are quite clear, human reason has often faltered in many ways and failed to see reality in its true perspective. It wandered off into deception after deception and the end result was nothing but confusion of thought and confusion in religion. History is proof enough of the errors of our ways.

Similarly, with regard to life after death, people have again put forward a host of competing notions; for instance, some have postulated that we are reduced to dust after death and will not rise to life again. Others have suggested that we are subject to a process of continuous reincarnation in this world and are punished or rewarded in the oncoming cycles of life by what we "come back as".

Even greater difficulty arises when we come to the question of what the right way to live is. To formulate a complete and balanced code of life that will conform to God's requirements, merely with the help of human reason, is an extremely difficult task. If a person is equipped with the highest faculties of reason and intellect and possesses matchless wisdom and the experience of many years of deliberation, even then the chances of his formulating an accurate view of the purpose of life and how to exist within it are not very promising. And even if, after a life spent in deliberation, he succeeds in doing that, he will still be plagued with nagging doubts about whether or not what he discovered about the truth and proper living is actually right.

Although it would have been the fairest and most realistic test of our wisdom, reason and knowledge to be left alone-with no guidance from God- and then to have had to discover the truth for ourselves and craft the most moral lifestyle on our own, thereby earning salvation, while all others would perish, thankfully, God has spared us such a hard test.

Through His grace and benevolence He chose for us people from among our own societies; people to whom He would reveal knowledge of the truth, of His attributes, His Law and the right way of living. He would also teach them about the meaning and purpose of life and of the afterlife as well. He would show them, so that they could show all the rest of us, the Divine-oriented lifestyle that leads to success in this life and eternal tranquility in the next. These chosen ones are the Messengers of God-His prophets. God has communicated knowledge and wisdom to them by means of inspiration, and any book containing a record of these Divine communications is called a Book of God, or a word of God.

Now the test of our wisdom and intellect lies in this: will we accept and take as our guide a professed Messenger of God, after thoroughly observing his pure and pious life and carefully studying his noble and flawless teachings? Anyone with any wisdom and sense would verify him as authentic and accept the instructions given by this Messenger of truth. If he denies the Messenger of God and his teachings, his denial would signify that he is devoid of the capacity to discover truth and righteousness. On account of this denial he would fail in his test. Such a one will never be able to uncover the truth about God and His Law and of the afterlife.

## Believing is not Always Seeing

As a matter of daily practice, whenever you need to find something out, you look for someone who can help you. But not just anybody will do. When you need to know accurate information you go to a source that you can trust and that can give you a measure of confidence. If you get sick and you aren't able to treat or cure yourself, you look for a doctor and accept and follow his or her instructions without question. Why? Because you know that he or she is properly qualified to give medical advice, has experience, and also has treated and cured many patients. So you'll follow their advice, implement the treatment plan prescribed and will avoid whatever they forbid.

Similarly, when it comes to the law you'll believe in whatever your legal advisers tell you and you'll act according to their instructions. In school you'll put your faith in your teacher or instructor and accept their lessons as true. If you want to travel somewhere, but don't know the way, you'll ask a perfect stranger for directions, and follow the way he points out.

In short, everyday when you want to know about something that would be either too difficult or impossible to find out on your own, you ask someone else and act accordingly. Your own knowledge base is inadequate so you carefully search for someone who can tell you the answer and then you silently accept their word. In a best case scenario you'll find an expert, rather than just an ordinary person who may know only a little of the topic you wish to explore. Then, after you've found your reliable source, you accept their advice unquestioningly.

This kind of faith, and that's really the right word for it, is called 'belief in what you cannot see', for you have relied on an expert's reputation and expertise without going through years of study and testing to acquire that expertise for yourself. Islam has a similar concept: there are things we cannot see or know about God by ourselves, but a reliable expert with a proven reputation is available to tell us about them.

Believing in what you cannot see means that you can gain knowledge of God, and spiritual matters, from someone who does know. You have never seen God, nor the full spectrum of His abilities and qualities. You don't see His angels directing the intricate forces that hold this universe together by His command, nor do you see them all around you. Just thinking about a Godly way of living won't result in your suddenly coming up with one yourself. You don't automatically know the details of the lifestyle that will make God happy with you and your left completely in the dark about the Afterlife and what's in it.

This kind of knowledge must come from the experts, from reliable people who know. This is where the concept of prophets comes in. They are people who have had direct contact with the Divine Being and have been endowed with certain knowledge. They are people whose sincerity, integrity, trustworthiness, godliness and absolute purity in their lives stand as irrevocable witness to the truth of their claim to knowledge. And above all, the very wisdom and force of their message makes you admit that they speak the truth and that their preaching deserves to be believed and followed.

This conviction of yours is literally 'believing in what you cannot see.' Having this kind of investigative and accepting attitude is essential for obedience to God, and for acting in accordance with His pleasure, for you have no other source than God's Messenger for accurate information, and without accurate and true information you cannot proceed properly on the path of submission to Him.

# 3

# Prophets

In the previous two chapters we have made clear the following points:

1.  The only way that we should properly order our lives is in obedience to God. Obedience, however, requires both knowledge and faith. As for knowledge, we must come to know something about God's basic nature and His attributes, as well as His likes and dislikes, the lifestyle He prefers for us to follow and also we must learn about the Day of Judgment. When faith in the truth and validity of those teachings is proved within our hearts, then faith is the result.

2.  Secondly, God has graciously spared us the arduous task of acquiring this knowledge through our personal efforts alone. He chose not to give us such an impossible task. Instead, He has revealed this knowledge to prophets, chosen from amongst humanity, and has commanded them to convey the Will of God to all who will listen in order to show them the right path. This act of grace has the potential to save many of us from formidable misfortunes.

3.  Lastly, the duty of men and women everywhere is to seek out news of a prophet and, after ascertaining that they have found one who must be a true prophet of God, to have faith in him and follow in his footsteps. This is the road to salvation. In this chapter we will be discussing the nature, history, and qualities of prophethood.

## What is a Prophet?

You can see that God has graciously provided us with all that we need to survive in this universe. Every newborn child arrives in the world endowed with eyes to see, ears to hear, a nose to smell and breathe, hands to touch, feet to walk, and a mind to think and ponder. All those potential abilities, skills, and faculties that a person needs or will need are carefully provided and marvelously set in his or her tiny body. Every possible requirement is foreseen and provided for. Excepting unforeseen medical complications, nothing that a child needs to grow is left out.

The same situation applies to the world that the child will live in. Everything essential for life is provided here in abundance: air, light, heat, etc. The child, even before opening his eyes, finds his first food nearby in his mother's breast. His parents love him instinctively and in their heart has been implanted an irresistible urge to look after him, to bring him up and to sacrifice their all for his welfare. Under the sheltering care of this constant nurturing, the child will slowly grow to maturity, and in every stage of his life, he will get from nature everything that he needs. All the material conditions for survival and growth are provided for and he may even think one day that the entire universe seems to be at his service.

Furthermore, every individual is blessed with all of those abilities, skills, and tools- physical, mental, and moral- which he will need in his struggle for life. In this, however, we find that God has made a seemingly uneven distribution. Indeed, He didn't endow each of us with identical capacities and abilities. Some are handicapped to one degree or another while others have differing mental capacities. If He would have given everyone the exact same set of physical and mental specifications, then people would never need each other. The beautiful principle of mutual care and cooperation would have been all but non-existent.

So, although the human race has practically everything it needs to survive (and also sufficient resources to look after its weaker members,) the implication is that among people individual characteristics vary widely. Some possess physical strength and prowess; others distinguish themselves for their mental talents. Some are born with greater aptitude for the arts, poetry, and philosophy; some possess a quick wit, while others have military skills, commercial intelligence, mathematical reasoning, scientific curiosity, literary observation, or a philosophic disposition.

These special aptitudes make each of us unique and enable us to grasp intricacies which may elude the mind of the average person. These insights, aptitudes and talents are gifts from God. They are embedded in the nature of those people whom God has destined to be thus distinguished. They are mostly inborn and cannot be acquired merely be education and training.

Careful reflection upon this disposition of God's gifts also reveals that these talents have been distributed amongst people in a marvelous way. Whatever general capabilities that are essential for human culture to survive are found generally within all people, while highly extraordinary talents which are needed only during highly unusual events are given only to a small number of people. The number of soldiers, farmers, artisans, and workers is large; but military generals, scholars, statesmen, and intellectuals are comparatively fewer.

The same is true of all professions, the arts and the icons of popular culture. The general rule seems to be that the greater the skill and genius, the fewer will be those who possess them. Super geniuses, who leave an indelible mark upon human history and whose achievements have guided humanity for ages, are few and far between. They are quite rare.

Here we are faced with another question: Is the fundamental need of human culture confined only to the need of having experts and specialists in the fields of law, politics, science, mathematics, engineering, mechanics, finance and economics and the like, or does it also need those who can show other people the way to

God and salvation? Temporal experts provide us with the knowledge of all that is in the world and of the ways and means to use it, but there must be someone to tell us the answers to questions like these: What is the purpose of creation and the meaning of life itself? What are we and why have we been created? Who has provided us with all the abilities we have and the resources we need to survive and why? What are the proper goals of life and how are they to be achieved? What are the best values to abide by and how can they be realized?

This kind of information will fulfill the most pressing need of humanity and unless we know these answers we will never be able to build a truly noble culture on a solid foundation and we will never really succeed in life, either here or in the hereafter. Our power of reason, itself, refuses to accept that God, Who has provided us with even the most trivial of our needs, would fail to provide for this greatest, most important and most vital need. No, it can never be so. And it is not so.

While God has produced people of distinction in the arts and sciences, He has also raised others who are possessed of a deep vision, pure intuition, and the highest abilities to know and understand Him. He revealed to them the way of godliness, piety, and righteousness. He gave them knowledge of the best goals of life and also of the values of morality and entrusted them with the duty to communicate the Divine Revelation to other human beings in order to show them the right path. These people are the Prophets and Messengers of God.

These prophets are distinguished from others in human society by their special talents, their natural mental disposition and their focused attitude towards life, just as experts in fields such as the arts and sciences are a breed apart from others. A person's own talent is their own advertisement and automatically persuades others to recognize it. When we listen to a born poet, we can immediately sense his special gift. Even if they try their absolute best, people who don't have the 'gift' of poetry will never succeed in moving others the way a master of the art can. The same is true of a great public speaker, writer, leader and inventor.

> **"There are three actions that are especially pleasing to God: serving Him and acknowledging that He has no equals; remaining firm in your faith and letting nothing divide you."**
>
> -Prophet Muhammad, peace be upon him

Every talent distinguishes itself by its remarkable ability and extraordinary achievements. Other, lesser qualified people just cannot stand up in comparison. The same holds true for a prophet. His mind grasps issues which defy other minds. He speaks and throws a rare light on subjects upon which no one else can speak. He has insight into subtle and intricate questions that no other would be able to understand even if they spent years in deep thought and meditation.

Reason accepts whatever he says; the heart knows its own truth. The experiences and observations of things in this world all point to the truth of every word that flows from his mouth. If we try, ourselves, to make up something just as profound, we find failure at every turn. A prophet's nature and character are so noble and pure that no matter what the situation, he maintains an attitude of honesty, integrity and nobility. He never does anything immoral nor does he tell lies. He always inspires people to be moral and good. More importantly, he practices what he preaches. His whole life is a testament to his harmonious relationship with his ideals.

Neither his word nor his deed is prompted by any self-interest. He suffers for the good of others, and never makes others suffer for his own good. His whole life is an example of truth, nobility, purity of nature, high thinking, and the very pinnacle of what it means to be a true human. His character is without any blemish and even the closest scrutiny fails to reveal any flaw in his life. And all these facts, all these attributes, make it evident that he is a prophet of God and that faith must be placed in his words.

When it becomes crystal clear that such a person is a true prophet of God, the logical course of action is that his words should be accepted, his instructions followed, and his orders, obeyed. It doesn't make sense to accept a person as God's true prophet, and then not believe in what he says or follow what he explains and models for us, for your very acceptance of him as God's prophet means that you've acknowledged that what he says is from God, and that whatever actions he does are in accordance with God's Will and pleasure.

Now, to disobey him is to disobey God- and disobedience to God leads to nothing but ruin and devastation. Therefore, the very acceptance of the prophet makes it incumbent upon all of us to bow to his instructions and accept them without any hesitation whatsoever. We might not always be able to understand the wisdom and usefulness of this or that order, but the very fact that an instruction has emanated from the Prophet is sufficient guarantee for its truth, and there can be no room for doubt or suspicion.

Our inability to understand sometimes doesn't mean that there is a flaw or defect with the teachings; for a common person's reasoning skills are not flawless in themselves. They have their own limitations and they cannot be ignored altogether. It's pretty clear that if someone doesn't know much about a topic, then they probably won't know about its finer points as well. A lay person would be a fool to reject what an expert says, merely with the excuse that he himself does not fully understand the concepts. It is worth noting that in every important worldly affair an expert is needed for advice, and when you turn to the expert you thereafter trust his advice and entirely depend upon it. You give up your own right of judgment and inference and follow him faithfully. Every ordinary person cannot be a master of all the arts and sciences of the world.

The best thing that an average person can do is to do the best that he can in whatever he is able and, in those things that are beyond his capacity, to use all his wisdom and shrewdness to seek out the proper guide and ask him for help. After finding this guide, he should accept his advice and follow him. When you are sure that a certain person is the best one available for your purpose, you ask his advice and guidance, and then trust in him. To interfere with him at every little step and say, "Help me to understand it before you proceed any further," is really imprudent.

When you engage a lawyer in any legal case, you don't interfere with him at every turn and pass. Rather, you put your faith in him and follow his instructions. When you need medical treatment you go to a doctor and follow his instructions. You neither poke your nose in medical matters nor test your skill in logic by debating with the doctor. This sense of knowing when something is beyond your skill, and having respect for those who are better equipped to handle it, is the proper attitude that one should have in daily life.

The same attitude must prevail with regards to religion also. You need the knowledge of God; you require information about how to live life according to God's pleasure; and you have no way of obtaining this knowledge by your own devices. It is incumbent upon you, therefore, to look for an authentic prophet of God. In your quest you will have to exercise the utmost care, discernment, and sagacity, for if you mistake an imposter for a true prophet, he will put you on the wrong track. If, however, after properly weighing and measuring all factors, you are convinced that a certain person is really God's prophet, then you must trust him completely and obey all his instructions faithfully.

Now it will become clear that the right path to follow is what that prophet teaches, and that the only correct way of life for us is the lifestyle he says is from God. From this we can easily understand that to have faith in the prophet and to obey and follow him is absolutely necessary for all people, and that a person who puts aside the prophet's instructions, and who tries to craft a devout way of life for himself, deviates from the right path and is almost certainly in danger of going astray.

In this matter people can be guilty of some really strange errors. There are people who admit the integrity and truthfulness of the prophet, but then they don't have faith in him, nor do they follow him in their worldly affairs. Such people are not only concealers of the truth, but also behave in a thoughtless and unnatural way: for not following a prophet, after admitting that he is authentic, means that one knowingly follows falsehood. And what folly can be greater than that!

Some people say, "We don't need a prophet to guide us. We can find out the way to truth ourselves." This, too, is a faulty attitude. Consider the following example: You've probably learned something about geometry at some point in your life, and you know that the shortest distance between two points, say A and B, can only be a straight line. All other lines out from A will have to bend or curve at some point on their journey to B, or they will fail to meet their mark. The same is the case with our journey towards the universal truth, which, in the terminology of Islam, is called the Straight Path. This path begins from each member of humanity and goes straight to God, and this path is a straight line; all other paths are crooked, bent or curved and will most likely lead the hapless traveler astray. This Straight Path has been specified by the Prophet, and there is and can be no straighter path besides that.

The one who ignores that direct path and seeks other side roads is only being fooled by his own imagination. He either constructs a new one or chooses some existing belief system and believes it to be right, but he soon finds himself entangled and lost in the mazes and meanderings created by his own fancy. What else can you think about a person who, having lost his way, ignores the guidance of a good man, saying to him, "I will not take your guidance nor accept the way you have shown to me, instead I will grope along in this unknown region and try to reach the object of my search, in my own way"? This attitude, when the clear guidance of the prophets is just waiting for him to take, is sheer stupidity. If everyone tries to reinvent the wheel, it would be a tremendous waste of time and energy. We never do so in the arts and sciences; so why in religion?

This call to self-reliance in seeking God is a common error, and even the smallest amount of reflection reveals its flaws and weaknesses. But if you go a little deeper into the matter, you will see that a person who rejects faith in a true prophet can't seem to find any straight or alternative route to God. That's because a person who refuses to believe the advice of a truthful man adopts such a perverse attitude that the vistas of truth become estranged from him and he becomes a victim of his own stubbornness, arrogance, bias, and perversity.

Often this refusal is because of arrogance, or blind conservatism or stubborn adherence to the ways of one's own forefathers, or it can be caused by a kind of slavery to the earthly desires that can overwhelm us, whose gratification becomes impossible by submission to the teachings of the prophets. If a person is entangled in any of the above conditions, the path to truth might close to him. He is like a person wearing stained glasses who can't see the true colors that are all around him. Such a person can't discover the road to salvation.

On the other hand, if a person is sincere and truth-loving and if he is not a slave to any of the above complexes, the road to reality becomes easy for him, and there are absolutely no grounds for him to refuse to believe in the prophet. On the contrary, he finds in the teachings of the prophet the very echo of his own soul and he discovers himself through discovering the prophet, for above all, God Himself is the One Who raised the true prophet to begin with. He is the One Who sent him to humanity to convey His message to His people. It's His Command to put faith in the prophet and to follow him. Thus, the one who refuses to believe in God's Messenger actually refuses to follow God's Commandments and becomes a rebel.

There is no denying the fact that a person, who refuses to acknowledge the authority of the representative of a king, is actually refusing the authority of the king, himself. This blatant disobedience turns him into a rebel. God is the Lord of the Universe, the true King, the very King of kings, and it is the duty of every human being to acknowledge the authority of His Messengers and Prophets and to obey them as His accredited representatives. Anyone who turns away from a Prophet of God is surely a concealer of truth, whether he claims he believes in God or not.

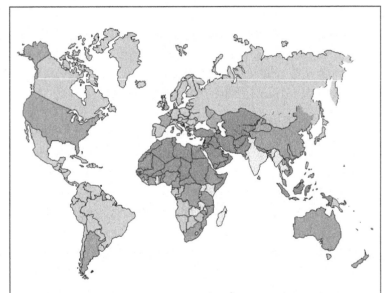

**Muslims live all over the world, with the greatest concentrations being in the Middle East, Asia, Africa and Europe.**

# The Prophets of Old

Now let's take a brief look at the history of prophethood. Let's see how this long chain began, how it gradually unfolded itself and finally, how it culminated in the prophethood of the last of the prophets, Muhammad (peace be upon him).

The entire human race springs from one original man and one original woman. We know their names as Adam and Eve. It was from them that the family of man grew and the human race multiplied. Science, using advanced DNA evidence, has corroborated that all human beings alive today are descended from one pair of ancestors who lived about 60,000 years ago or more in Africa. So history, science and religion can agree on this crucial point.

Adam, the first man on earth, was also appointed by God to be His first Prophet. God revealed His rules about living life on earth properly to Adam and enjoined him to convey and communicate this message (i.e. Islam) to his descendants. These teachings would include the following: to teach them that Allah is One, the Creator, and Sustainer of the world; that He is the Lord of the universe and that He alone should be served and obeyed; that to Him they will have to return one day and to Him alone they should appeal for help; that they should live good, pious, and righteous lives in accordance with God's pleasure and that if they did so they would be blessed by God with a fantastic reward, and if they turned away from Him and disobeyed Him that they would be losers here and in the hereafter and would be severely punished for this disbelief and disobedience.

Those of Adam's descendants who were mindful lived by the right path shown to them by him, but those who were inclined to sinfulness eventually abandoned their father's teachings, and gradually drifted off into devious ways. Since the hand of a supernatural force is clearly evident in the intricate web of life and in our environment around us, even people who cover over the truth of the One God will soon seek an object of devotion.

So some of those who went off the path began to worship the sun, the moon, and the stars; others took to the worship of trees, animals, and rivers. Some believed that air, water, fire health, and all the blessings and forces of Nature were each under the control of a different god and that each one of them should be placated through worship. In this way ignorance gave rise to many forms of polytheism and idolatry, and scores of man-made religions were invented. This age of division and religious creativity followed the path of Adam's progeny as they spread out all over the globe and formed different races and nations.

Every nation made a different religion for itself, each with formalities and rituals of its own. God, the one Lord and Creator of humanity and the universe, was altogether forgotten. Not only that, Adam's descendants forgot even the way of life which God had revealed for them and which their great ancestor had taught them. They followed their own guidelines, thus every kind of evil custom grew, and all sorts of notions of ignorance spread them. They also began to err in discerning right from wrong. Many immoral practices began to be considered right and many right things were not only ignored but dubbed as wrong.

In time, after humanity was nearly lost, God began to raise prophets among every people, who preached Islam to them. Each one reminded his people of the lessons their ancestors had forgotten. They taught them to serve only the One God, to put an end to idol-worship and to the practice of associating other deities with God. Not only that, but they also fought against all the old customs of ignorance, taught them the right way of living in accordance with God's pleasure, and gave them life-affirming laws to be followed and enforced in society for the good of all. God's true Prophets were raised in all regions, in every land and for every people. They all possessed one and the same religion, the religion of Islam, i.e. submission to God's Will.

No doubt, the methods of teaching and the legal codes of the different Prophets were a little different in accordance with the needs and the stage of culture of the people among whom they were raised. Indeed, the particular teachings of each prophet were determined by the kinds of evils which he faced and endeavored to eradicate. The methods of reform also differed as needed to alter the different erroneous notions and ideas that were prevalent in that particular prophet's society.

When any given tribe or community of people were in a primitive stage of social development, civilization and intellectual achievement, their laws and regulations were simple; they were modified and improved as the society evolved and progressed. These differences were, however, only superficial and cursory. The fundamental teachings of all these expressions of religion were the same, i.e. belief in the unity of God, adherence to a life of piety, goodness and peace, and belief in a life after death with its fair process for reward and punishment.

**The name "Allah" (God) written in Arabic**

# Prophets and Islam

All Prophets taught Islam. This may sound like a strange notion, but if you merely translate the meaning of the word Islam, "submission to God and peace", then one can reasonably assert that, yes, all Prophets taught the same thing. They were all Muslims.

Prophets are sinless. What does this mean? All people are capable of sin, right? While this is true, before God pours forth His Guidance into the heart of a human being, that heart must first be cleansed of any taint of sin. God purifies the Prophets from sin and thereafter we call them sinless. While they still can make mistakes and errors of judgment in their later life, they never commit a sin again as their hearts have been immunized from any desire to do so.

Where are their messages? Most prophets lived in societies with no system of writing. Their messages were thus brief and oral in nature- the most susceptible to being changed from one generation to the next. A few prophets received messages that were organized, codified and could be permanently recorded. These "Books of God" or scriptures were not immune to being lost or corrupted, either, but some have partially survived in one form or another to this day.

The teachings of the Jewish prophets are still scattered throughout the Old Testament, while some of the authentic words of Jesus can be uncovered in the Gospels through careful examination. Other ancient civilizations such as the Sumerians, the Egyptians and the early Chinese dynasties mention intriguing examples of what may be the scattered remnants of the words of authentic prophets

Humanity's attitude towards God's Prophets has been strange, however. First of all, many communities have often mistreated the prophets and refused to listen and accept their teachings. Some of the prophets were expelled from their lands; some were assassinated;

some, in the face of their people's indifference, continued preaching their whole lives, and hardly won more than a few followers.

In the midst of this fierce opposition, derision, and indignity to which they were perpetually subjected, these Apostles of God, however, did not cease to preach. Their patient determination almost always succeeded: their teachings made some kind of effect in the end. Many people and even nations accepted their message and were converted to their creed. But the tendency of people to deviate, born of centuries of practice in cultural evolution, ignorance, and malpractice, now took another form. Even though they accepted and practiced the teachings of their prophets during their lifetimes, yet after their guides died, within a few generations they wove their old distorted notions back into their new religions, making a synthesis of the two and altering the prophet's original teachings in the process.

How did this manifest itself? One way was in adopting unusual methods for worshipping God, like engaging in bizarre rituals or adopting magic talismans or totems. Other people might take to worshipping their prophets as gods themselves! Some made their prophets out to be incarnations of God on earth, while yet others turned their prophets into sons of God. Many more have associated their prophets with God in His Divinity, making something of a multi-faced kind of god.

In short, humanity's varied attitudes in this respect were a travesty of his reason and a mockery of himself;

he made idols of those very people whose holy mission was to smash idols to pieces. By intermixing religion, custom, ignorant rituals, baseless and false anecdotes and man-made laws, people so changed and perverted the ideology of the prophets that after the passage of many centuries it became a mixture of the real and the fictitious.

The original teachings of the prophets were lost in a conglomeration of fantasies and perversities so much so that it becomes impossible to distinguish the wheat from the chaff. And, not content with this corruption of the prophet's message, they further attached made-up legends and unworthy traditions to the lives of their prophets and so corrupted their life histories that a real and reliable account of their lives becomes impossible to be discerned.

Despite these mistakes carried out by their followers through the ages, the work of the prophets has not been altogether pointless. Among all nations, in spite of all the interpolation and alteration, some traces of Truth have survived. The idea of God and of a life after death has been definitely assimilated in some form or other in all religions. A few principles of goodness, truth and morality are commonly agreed upon throughout the whole world. The prophets, thus, prepared the mental attitude of their respective people in such a way that a universal religion could be safely introduced- a religion, which is in absolute harmony with the nature of humanity, which embodies all that is good in all other creeds and cultures, and which is naturally and commonly acceptable to the entire world.

As we have said above, in the early days of humanity separate prophets used to appear among different nations or groups of people, and the teachings of each prophet were meant especially and specifically for his own people. The reason was that at that stage of history, nations were situated separately and were so cut off from each other that one was bound up within the geographical limits of its own territories and the facilities for mutual intercourse were completely non-existent. In such circumstances it was very difficult to propagate a common world faith with its accompanying system of living life in this world uniformly. Besides, the general conditions of the early nations were widely different from one another.

**This artwork is fancy calligraphy that reads:**
**"There is no god but Allah,**
**and Muhammad is the Messenger of Allah."**

70

Their ignorance was great, and among the different peoples it had given rise to different forms of moral aberration and distortions of faith. It was, therefore, necessary that different prophets be raised to preach the Truth to them and win them over to God's ways, to gradually eradicate evils and aberrations, to root out the ways and modes of ignorance and teach them to practice the noblest principles of simple, pious, and righteous living, and thus to train and bring them up in the arts and crafts of moral living. God alone knows how many thousands of years were spent in developing humanity mentally, morally, and spiritually. In any case, humanity continued to make progress and at last the time came when they grew from their infancy, and entered the age of maturity.

With the progress and spread of commerce, industry and the arts, communication was established between the far flung nations of the earth. From China and Japan, to the distant reaches of Europe and Africa, regular trade routes were opened both by sea and land. Many people learnt the art of writing and many other types of knowledge spread. Ideas also began to travel from one country to another and learning and scholarship began to be exchanged. Great conquerors appeared, extended their conquests far and wide, established vast empires, and knit many different nations under unified political systems. Thus nations came closer and to one another, and their differences became fewer.

# All Religions have a Common Root

"Be patient with those who behave foolishly towards you; forgive those who wrong you; give unto those who deny you; and strengthen your ties with those who break away from you."

-Muhammad

"But I tell you not to resist an evil person. But whoever slaps you on your right cheek, turn the other to him also."

-Jesus Christ

"Hatred is not ended by more hatred."

-Buddha

It became possible under these circumstances that one unified faith, encompassing a comprehensive and all-embracing way of life, catering to the moral, spiritual, social, cultural, political, economic, and all other needs of humanity and embodying both religious and secular elements could be sent by God for the entire world. More than two thousand years ago humanity had attained a mental disposition that seemed to crave a universal religion. Buddhism emerged from India and spread as far as Japan on one side, and to Afghanistan, on the other. Though it consisted of some noble moral principles, it was soon corrupted with idolatry as

Buddha was elevated into a god. With the resulting superstitions and falsifications added to it, it failed as a complete system of life.

A few centuries later, a new light appeared in the Middle East in the person of Jesus, the Messiah (peace be upon him). Although the religion he taught was equivalent to Islam, his followers wound up reducing it to nothing more than a mixture of paganism, Judaism and some of their master's original traditions, resulting in a fractious blend called Christianity. Even this jumbled up faith spread into far off places from Persia and Asia Minor in the east to the distant reaches of both Europe and Africa.

From these events it is clearly inferred that the conditions of humanity in that age demanded a common religion for the whole human race and that the world was so prepared for it that when they found no complete and true religion in existence, they began to propagate among the nations the prevalent religions, no matter how defective, incomplete, or unsatisfying they might come to be.

At such a crucial stage of human civilization, when the mind of humanity was itself craving for a world religion, a prophet was raised in Arabia for the whole world and for all nations. The religion he was given to propagate was again, Islam, but now it would be given in the form of a complete and full-fledged system, covering all aspects of the individual and material life of humanity. He was made a prophet for the entire human race and was told to propagate his mission to the whole world. He was Muhammad, the Prophet of Islam, peace be upon him.

## Muhammad as Prophet

If we take a look at the world in an atlas, we find that no other country could have been more suitable for the much needed world religion than Arabia. It is situated right in between Africa and Asia and is the crossroads for lands further beyond each. At the time of Muhammad's appearance southern Europe was blessed with a civilized and culturally advanced atmosphere, still influenced as it was by the echoes of the great Roman Empire; and India, just beyond Persia, also had benefited from many centuries of development. Arabia was the link in the chain of trade and cultural diffusion that tied both together.

Now look at the history of that time period, centering on the sixth century, and you will find that no other people were more suited for the endowment of this task of accepting and promulgating the message of a last, world-wide message than the Arabs. The great nations of the world had been struggling hard for world supremacy, and in this long struggle and incessant strife, they had exhausted all their resources and vitality. The Arabs were a fresh and virile people. The meandering social development of the more advanced cultures had produced a curious mix of both good and bad morals and practices which persisted from generation to generation. These included such oddities as despotism, monarchies, exploitation of peasants, gluttony and the like.

Among the Arabs, however, no such far reaching social organization existed, and they were, therefore, free from the inactivity, debasement and indulgences arising out of luxury, poor government and sensual satiety. The pagan Arabs of the fifth century had not been affected by the evil influence of the artificial systems and civilizations of the great nations of the world.

Though far from being perfect people, as banditry, idolatry, abject slavery, and chauvinism existed in their peninsula, nevertheless, they were possessed of a remarkable array of noble qualities, which people untouched by the 'moral laxity' of the time, ought to possess. They were brave, fearless, generous, faithful to their promises, lovers of freedom, and were politically independent -not subject to the control of any imperial powers. They lived a very simple life, and were strangers to the life of luxury and over-indulgence.

As mentioned previously, there were certain undesirable aspects of their culture as well, as we shall explore later on, but the reason for the existence of such bad qualities was for the reason that for thousands of years no prophet had arisen among them, nor had there appeared a reformer who might have civilized them and purged their moral life of all evil impurities. Centuries of free and independent life in sandy deserts had bred and nourished extreme ignorance among them. They had, therefore, become so hard-hearted and firm in their traditions of ignorance that to make them more civilized was not the task of an ordinary man.

At the same time, however, they did possess a potential quality that could be activated by some person of extraordinary influence. If he were to invite them to reform, and give them a noble ideal and a complete program to follow, they would accept his call and readily rise to work for the achievement of that goal. Further still, they would spare no effort or sacrifice to advance the cause. They would be prepared to face, without the least hesitation, even the hostility of the entire world in the furtherance of their mission. It was just such a young, forceful, and virile nation that was needed for disseminating the teachings of the world prophet: Muhammad (Peace be upon him).

Can evidence for their readiness be found in their very language itself? When we look to the Arabic language and study it and delve deeply into its literature, we would soon be convinced that there is no other language than Arabic which is more suited to give expression to universal ideals, to explain the most delicate and subtle problems of Divine knowledge, and to impress the heart of man and mold it into God's submission.

Small phrases and brief sentences express a world of ideas, and at the same time they are so forceful that they steal into the heart; their every sound has the potential to move people to tears and ecstasy. They are so sweet that it is felt as if honey were being poured into the ears; they are so full of harmony that every fiber of the listener's body is moved by their symphony. A rich and powerful language was needed for the Qur'an, the exalted Word of God. It was, therefore, the manifestation of God's great wisdom that He chose the land of Arabia for the birth place of the world prophet. Let us now look into the personality and uniqueness of the man chosen by God for this mission of being the last prophet for the entire world.

## The Rational Proof for Prophethood

If one were to close one's eyes and imagine oneself in the world of 1500 years ago, one would find that it was a world completely different from ours, having not even the least semblance to the fast-paced and interconnected world that we find around ourselves today. How few and far between were the opportunities for the exchange of ideas! How limited and undeveloped were the means of communication! How little and meager was humanity's knowledge! How narrow was their outlook! How wrapped up were they in superstition and oddball ideas!

Ignorant darkness was the order of the day. There was only the faintest glimmer of learning, which could hardly brighten the horizon of human knowledge. There were neither computers nor cell phones, televisions nor movies. Trains and cars and airplanes were undreamt of, and printing presses and bookstores were unknown.

Hand-written tomes by lone authors or the expensive work of copyists was all that there was to supply whatever scanty literary material there was available to be transmitted from generation to generation. Education, such as it was, was a luxury, meant only for the most fortunate, and educational institutions were practically non-existent.

The collected compilation of human knowledge was small, humanity's outlook was narrow, and people's ideas about life and the world around them were confined by their limited surroundings. Even a scholar of that age lacked much of the knowledge possessed by the average person of today, and the most cultured person was less refined than our own neighbors in the street. Indeed, humanity was steeped in ignorance and superstition. Whatever light of learning there was seemed to be fighting a losing battle against the darkness prevailing all around.

What are considered to be matters of common knowledge today could hardly be acquired in those days even after years of calculated thought and patient research. People used to undertake hazardous journeys and spent a whole lifetime in acquiring that modest information which is everybody's heritage in the present age of learning. Things, which are classified as 'myth' and 'superstition' today, were the unquestionable truths of that age. Acts, which we now regard as cruel and barbarous, were then the order of the day.

Everyday values practiced back then, which appear obnoxious to our moral sense today, constituted the very heart of proper conduct back then. Skepticism had reached such epidemic proportions that people refused to consider anything as timeless truth and verified fact unless it came in the form of the supernatural, the extraordinary, the uncanny, and even the illogical. They developed such an inferiority complex that they could never imagine a human being to possess a godly soul or a saint to be a mere human.

## In the Dark: Arabia before Islam

In that age of ignorance, there was a land where darkness lay even heavier and thicker. The neighboring countries of Persia, Byzantium and Egypt possessed a glimmer of civilization and the faint light of learning. But Arabia could not benefit from their cultural influences. It stood isolated, cut off by vast oceans of sand and surrounded on three sides by water. Arab traders traveled great distances, which often took them on months long journeys, to carry their wares to and from these countries, but they could hardly acquire any grain of knowledge on their travels. In their own country, they did not have a single educational institution or library.

None seemed to be interested in the cultivation and advancement of knowledge. The few who were literate were not educated enough to have anything to do with the existing arts and sciences. They did possess a highly developed language capable of expressing the finest shades of human thought in a remarkable manner. They also possessed an oral literary taste of high order. But the study of the remnants of their surviving oral tradition reveals how limited was their knowledge, how low was their standard of culture and civilization, how saturated were their minds with superstitions, how barbarous and ferocious were their thoughts and customs, and how uncouth and degraded were their moral standards and conceptions.

It was a country without a government; every tribe claimed sovereignty and considered itself to be an independent entity. There was no law except the law of the jungle. Looting, arson, and the murder of innocents and the poor were the order of the day. Life, property, and honor were constantly at stake. The various tribes were always a moment away from drawing swords against each other. Any trivial incident was enough to cause an explosion of ferocious fury, which sometimes even developed into a region-wide conflict which could last for several decades. Indeed, a bedouin would not even consider showing mercy to an enemy tribesman, whom, he thought, he had every right to kill and rob.

Whatever notions they had of morals, culture, and civilization, were primitive and uncouth. They could hardly discriminate between pure and impure, lawful and unlawful, civil and uncivil. Their life was wild, their methods were barbaric. They reveled in adultery, gambling and drinking. Loot and plunder was their motto, murder and rapine their very habits. They would stand stark naked before each other without any qualms of conscience.

Even their womenfolk would become nude during the ceremony of circling the Ka'bah. But the worst of it involved foolish notions of prestige: heads of families would bury their "surplus" baby girls alive in the desert lest anyone should become their son-in-law and divide their family fortune. Instead, they would marry their stepmothers after the death of their fathers. They were ignorant of even the rudiments of simple everyday routines such as proper manners in eating, dressing, and washing.

With regards to their religious beliefs, they suffered from the same shortcomings which were playing havoc with the rest of the world. They worshipped stones, trees, idols, stars, and elusive spirits. In short, everything conceivable except God. They did not know anything about the teachings of the prophets of old. They had an idea that Abraham and Ishmael were their forefathers, but they knew next to nothing about their religious teachings and about the God Whom their distant ancestors worshipped.

The stories of the ancient tribes of 'Ad and Thamud were to be found in their folklore, but they contained no traces of the teachings of Prophets Hud and Saleh. The Jews and the Christians had transmitted to them certain legendary folktales relating to the Israelite prophets, but they presented a rather bleak picture of those noble souls. Their stories were adulterated with the figments

81

of their own imagination and thus the tales of the prophets were filled with episodes of sin, immorality and weakness.

Even today, an idea can be had of the religious conceptions of those people by casting a cursory glance at those Israelite traditions which Muslim commentators of the Qur'an have conveyed to us. Indeed, the picture which has been presented there of the institution of prophethood and of the Israelite Prophets is the very antithesis of all that those noble followers of truth had stood for.

The Middle East in the 6th Century

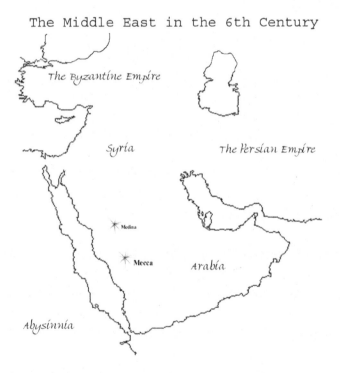

## Muhammad's Early Life

In such a dark age and in such a blighted country a man is born. In his early childhood both his parents die and, a few years later, the sad demise of his grandfather also occurs. Consequently, he is deprived of even that scant training and upbringing which an Arab child of his time could get. Though he lived in a thriving merchant town, in his boyhood he is made to tend flocks of sheep and goats in the hills with only the occasional company of an odd bedouin boy here and there. When he is on the cusp of manhood, he decides to enter the world of trade. All his friendships and dealings are with other Arabs. Education does not even touch him; he is completely illiterate and unschooled. He never even gets the chance to sit in the company of a learned scholar, for such men were almost totally non-existent in Arabia.

He does have two opportunities to go out of his country, but those journeys are confined to Syria and are nothing more than the usual business trips undertaken by Arab trade caravans. (The first trip at twelve years old saw him playing the role of a stable boy for his uncle's caravan, while the second trip in his early twenties saw him the manager of a caravan in the employ of an Arab businesswoman.) If he met any people in Syria or had the occasion to observe any aspects of culture and civilization, those random meetings and stray observations cannot be given any place in the making of his personality. For such things can never have that profound an influence upon anyone which may lift him totally out of his environment, transform him completely, and raise him to such heights of originality and glory that there remains no connection between him and the society he is born in.

Nor can two short caravan trips to southern Syria be the means for acquiring such a profound and vast knowledge that would transform an illiterate Arab into the leader not only of his own region and age, but of much of the world at large and for ages to come. Indeed, whatever the measure of the intellectual and cultural influence of those journeys one might suppose, the fact remains that they could in no way impart to him those conceptions and principles of religion, ethics, culture, and civilization which were totally nonexistent in his world in those days, and they could in no way create that sublime and perfect pattern of human character which was nowhere to be found in those days of uncouth manners and low social values.

## A Diamond in the Rough

Let us now look at the life and work of this noble man in the context not only of Arabian society but also of the entire world as it stood in that period.

Muhammad is totally different from the people among whom he is born and with whom he passes his youth and early manhood, until finally achieving his full stature. He has the uncontested reputation for never telling a lie. His entire community is unanimous in testifying to his honesty. Even his worst enemies never accuse him of telling a lie on any occasion whatsoever during his entire life. He talks politely and never uses obscene or abusive language. He has a charming personality and gentle manners about him.

In his dealings with other people he always follows the principles of justice and fair play. He engages in trade and commerce on and off for years, but never once participates in any dishonest transaction. Those who deal with him in business have full confidence in his integrity. His peers soon give him the nickname, "Al-Ameen," which means the Trustworthy.

Even those depraved individuals who dislike him for his integrity wind up depositing their costly belongings with him for safe keeping and he scrupulously fulfils their trust. He is the very embodiment of a gentleman in the midst of a society which is rotten to the core. Born and bred among a people who regard drunkenness and gambling as normal, he never touches alcohol and never indulges in gambling. His people are uncouth, uncultured and unclean, but he personifies in himself the highest culture and the most refined aesthetic outlook.

Surrounded on all sides by heartless people, he himself has a heart overflowing with the love of human kindness. He helps orphans and widows. He is hospitable to travelers. He brings harm to no one; rather, he goes all out to suffer hardships for others' sake. Living among those for whom war and banditry are good business, he is such a lover of peace that his heart aches for them when they take up arms and cut each other's throats. He keeps aloof from the feuds of his tribe, and is foremost in bringing about reconciliation.

Born among an idolatrous race, he is so clear-minded and possesses such a pure soul that he regards nothing in the heavens and the earth worth worshipping except the One True God Who cannot be seen. He does not bow before any created thing and does not partake of the offerings made to idols, even in his childhood. Instinctively, he hates any form of worship involving any creatures and beings besides God. In brief, the towering and radiant personality of this man in the midst of such a hopeless and backwards environment, may be likened to a light house beacon lighting a pitch-dark night or to a diamond shining in a heap of coal.

## A New Way Arises

After spending the greater part of his life in such a chaste, pure, and civilized manner there comes a revolution in his heart. He feels fed up with the darkness and ignorance massed all around him. He wants to steer clear of the horrible sea of backwardness, corruption, immorality, idolatry and disorder which surround him on all sides. He finds everything around him imbalanced and out of synch with his soul. He begins to take long walks into the hills, away from the hustle and bustle of town. He spends days and nights in perfect seclusion and meditation. He even begins to eat less so that

86

through hunger his soul and his heart may become purer and nobler still.

He muses and ponders deeply. He is in search of a light which can melt away the prevailing darkness. He becomes convinced that if he could just get hold of a force that could bring about the downfall of the corrupt and disorderly world of his day he could lay the foundations of a new and better world. But it all remains just a dream within a man who would be powerless to start such an agenda on his own.

A day comes, however, when his own mortal musings are interrupted- when a remarkable change overwhelms him. All of a sudden his heart is illuminated with the light of the Divine One, giving him the insight and capability he had always yearned for.

He comes out of the recesses of his mountain retreat, and then goes to his people and addresses them saying, "The idols that you worship are a mere sham. Stop worshipping them from now on. No mortal being, no star, no tree, no stone, no spirit, is worthy of human veneration. So don't bow your heads in worship before them.

The entire universe and everything it contains belongs only to God Almighty. He is the Creator, the Nourisher, the Sustainer, and the real Sovereign before Whom all should bow down and to whom all should pray and render obedience. So serve only Him and obey only His commands. Looting and plunder, murder and rape, injustice and cruelty- all the evils that you indulge in are crimes in the sight of God. Leave your evil ways. He hates all sin. Speak only the truth. Be just and fair with others. Don't murder anyone. Don't rob anyone. Take only what is yours, not what belongs to others. Pay what you owe to others fairly."

"You are human beings and all human beings are equal in the eyes of God. No one is born with the slur of shame on his face, nor has anyone come into the world with the crown of honor hung around his neck. The only one who is high and honored is the one who is God-fearing and pious, as well as true in words and deeds. Distinctions of birth and glory and of race are no standard for greatness and honor. The one who fears God and does good deeds is the noblest. The one who fears God and does good deeds is the noblest of human beings. The one who is bereft of the love of God and is steeped in bad manners is doomed."

"There is an appointed day after your death when you will have to appear before your Lord. You will be called to account for all your deeds, good or bad, and you won't be able to hide anything. Your whole life's work will be an open book to Him. Your fate will be determined by your faith first, followed by your record of good or bad actions. In the court of the all-knowing supreme Judge no doubts will arise. You won't be able to bribe Him. No consideration will be given to your pedigree or parentage. Only true faith and good deeds will give you status then. The one who will have enough of both requirements will take his place in Heaven and experience eternal happiness; while the one who has neither of them will be cast in the fire of Hell."

This is the message with which he comes, simple and clear, yet his ignorant people turn against him. Abuses and stones are showered upon his noble person. Every conceivable torture and cruelty is perpetrated upon him and his followers. And this continues, not just for a day or two, but without interruption for thirteen long and harrowing years. At last he goes into exile. But he is not given a break even there. He is hounded by the enemies he left behind in many ways in his place of refuge. The whole of Arabia is eventually incited against him. He is persecuted and pursued continuously for a full eight years there. But he suffers through it all; he doesn't budge an inch from the stand he has taken. He is resolute, firm and inflexible in his purpose and position.

## Why was He Opposed?

One may ask: how is it that his nation became his sworn enemy? Was there any dispute over gold and silver or other worldly possessions? Was it due to any blood feud? Did he ask for anything from them? No! The hatred was based on the fact that he had asked them to worship the One True God and to lead a life of righteousness, pity, and goodness. He had preached against idolatry and the worship of other beings besides God and had denounced their immoral way of life. He spoke out against the practice of venerating holy men.

He implored people passionately to give up the idea of upper and lower class boundaries in society, and had condemned the prejudices of clan and race as sheer ignorance; and he wanted to change the whole structure of society which had been handed down to them from time immemorial. In their turn, his countryman told him that the principles of his mission were hostile to their ancestral traditions and asked him either to shut up or to suffer the worst consequences.

One may ask: why did he suffer all those hardships, especially, as you will see, when he didn't have to, if he just would have compromised a bit? The leaders of his home town of Mecca offered to accept him as their king and to lay all the riches of the land at his feet if only he would give up preaching his religion and spreading his message. But he chose to refuse the tempting offers and to suffer for his cause, instead. Why? Was he to gain in any way if those people became pious, humble and righteous?

Why was it that he didn't care a bit for riches and luxury, kingship and glory, or ease and plenty? Was he making a bold play for some larger profits down the road that would make his initial offers seem so paltry? Were those supposed grander schemes so tempting that he would choose to go through fire and steel and weather countless tortures of the soul and body calmly and resolutely for years? One has to ponder over it deeply to find an answer.

Can anyone ever imagine a higher example of self-sacrifice, concern and kind-heartedness towards his fellow-beings than a man who would ruin his own happiness for the good of others, while those very people for whose sake he is striving ceaselessly, should stone him, give him no chance even in his exile, and that, after all this, he should never give up working for their well-being?

Would any insincere person undergo so much suffering for a false cause? Can any dishonest speculator and visionary exhibit such firmness and determination for his ideal as to stick to his guns to the very last and remain unruffled and unperturbed in the face of dangers and tortures of every conceivable description when a whole country rises up in arms against him?

This faith, this perseverance, and this resolution, with which he led his movement to ultimate success, is, therefore, an eloquent proof of the supreme truth of his cause. Had there been the slightest touch of doubt and uncertainty in his heart, he could never have been able to brave the storm which continued to fall in all its fury for over twenty long years. This is but one side of the revolution that sprang up in his heart. The other side is even more amazing and remarkable.

## Why the Sudden Mid-life Change?

For forty years he lived as an ordinary man among his fellow Arabs in Mecca. In that long period he was not known as a statesman, a preacher, or an orator. No one had ever heard of him imparting gems of wisdom and possessing the kind of knowledge that he suddenly had after becoming a prophet. Before prophethood he was never seen lecturing upon the principles of metaphysics, ethics, law, politics, economics, or sociology. After Islam came to him, he even displayed all the qualities of a great military general and tactician, and yet, before Islam, he wasn't even thought to have any ordinary fighting skill at all. Before prophethood he was never known to talk about God, angels, holy books, ancient prophets, old forgotten civilizations, judgment day, life after death, or heaven and hell.

No doubt he possessed an excellent character and charming manners, and was highly cultured, yet there was nothing so special and so radically extraordinary about him that would make others think that something great and revolutionary would come from him in the future. He was known among his acquaintances as a sober, calm, gentle, law-abiding citizen of good nature. But when he came out of his mountain retreat with a new message, he was completely transformed to a new spiritual and intellectual level.

When he began preaching his message soon the whole of Arabia stood in awe and wonder and was bewitched by his wonderful eloquence and oratory. It was so impressive and captivating that his worst enemies were afraid of hearing it, lest it should penetrate deep into the recesses of their hearts or the very marrow of their beings and carry them off their feet and make them bid goodbye to their old religion and culture. The message was so matchless that the whole legion of Arab poets, desert preachers, and orators of the highest talent failed to bring forth its equivalent in beauty of language and splendor of diction when he threw the challenge to his opponents to put their heads together and produce even a single line like the one he recited.

## How did His Message Change Everything?

Along with this, he now appeared before his people as a unique philosopher, a wonderful reformer, a renowned creator of culture and civilization, an illustrious politician, a great leader, a judge of the highest eminence and an incomparable general. This illiterate bedouin, this dweller of the desert, spoke with such learning and wisdom, the like of which none had said before and none could say after him.

He expounded upon the intricate problems of metaphysics and theology. He delivered speeches on the principles of the decline and fall of nations and empires, supporting his thesis by the historical data of the past. He reviewed the achievements of the old reformers, passed judgments on the various religions of the world, and gave verdicts on the differences and disputes between nations. He taught ethical canons and principles of culture. He formulated such laws of social culture, economic organization, group conduct, and international relations that even eminent thinkers and scholars can grasp their true wisdom only after life-long research and vast experience. Their beauties, indeed, unfold themselves progressively as humanity advances in theoretical knowledge and practical experience.

The Dome of the Rock, or *al-Quds* as it is known. This structure was built over the site where it is believed that Muhammad was taken on a spiritual journey to heaven.

This silent and peace-loving trader who had never handled a sword before, who had no military training, who had participated in a battle only once as a teenager, and that just as a spectator, turned suddenly into such a brave soldier that he did not even once retreat in the fiercest battles. He become such a great general that he conquered the whole of Arabia in nine years, at a time

94

when the weapons of war were primitive and the means of communication poor.

His military skill and efficiency developed to such a high degree, and the military spirit and principles which he imparted to a motley crowd of Arabs (who had no equipment worth the name) wrought such a miracle that within a few years they overthrew the two most formidable military empires of the day and became the masters of the greater part of the then known world.

This reserved and quiet man who, for a full forty years never gave any indication of any political interest or activity, suddenly appeared on the stage of the world as such a great political reformer and statesman that, without the aid of radio, satellites or even a printing press, he brought together the scattered inhabitants of a desert encompassing thousands of square miles, and took a people who were warlike, ignorant, unruly, uncultured, and plagued by constant tribal warfare- and united them under one banner, one law, one religion, one culture, one civilization, and one form of government.

He changed the way they thought about the world, even their very habits and morals. He turned the ill-mannered into the cultured, the barbarous into the civilized, sinners and bad characters into pious, God-fearing, and righteous people. Their unruly and stiff-necked natures were transformed into models of obedience and submission to law and order. A nation which had not produced a single great man worth the name for centuries gave birth, under his influence and guidance, to thousands of noble souls who went forth to the far-off corners of the world to preach and teach the principles of religion, morals and civilization.

He accomplished this feat not through any worldly bribes or through oppression or cruelty, but by his captivating manners, his endearing moral personality, and his convincing ways. With his noble and gentle behavior he befriended even his enemies. He captured the hearts of the people with his unbounded sympathy and depth of his humanity.

He ruled justly; he wouldn't even think to swerve from truth and righteousness. He never oppressed anyone, even his deadly enemies who were out for his blood, who had pelted him with stones, who had turned him out of his native home, who had goaded the whole of Arabia against him. No, not even those who had chewed the raw liver of his dead uncle in a frenzy of vengeance. He forgave them all when he triumphed over them. He never took revenge on anyone for his personal grievances or the wrongs done against him.

Besides the fact that he became the ruler of his country, he was so selfless and modest that he remained very simple and frugal in his habits. In his daily life he lived as if he were a poor man, as before, in his humble thatched mud cottage. He slept on an uncomfortable mattress made of palm leaves, wore rough clothes, ate the simplest food, and sometimes went without any food at all. He used to spend whole nights standing in prayer before his Lord.

He came to the rescue of the poor and the desperate. He never had any problem with doing the work of a common laborer. Until his last moments there was not the slightest hint of royal pride or the haughtiness of the high and the rich in him. Like an ordinary man he would sit and walk with people and share their joys and sorrows. He would mingle so frequently in public crowds that a visiting stranger would often find it difficult to distinguish the leader of the nation from the rest of the people in the street.

In spite of his greatness, his behavior with the humblest person was that of an ordinary human being. In the struggles and endeavors of his whole life he did not seek any reward or profit for his own person, nor did he allow any property to be left for his heirs. He dedicated his all to community. He was so concerned that his followers not earmark anything for him or his descendants that he specifically forbade his descendants from receiving the benefit of any government collected charity, lest his followers in the future decide to give them a share.

An aerial view of Mecca in Arabia. The black cube-shaped building in the middle of the plaza is the *Ka'bah*, a shrine believed to have been first built by Abraham.

Note the barren ruggedness of the surrounding land. The entire plaza complex is known as the Masjid Al Haram, or the Sanctified Mosque.

## What New Ideas Did He Bring?

The achievements of this great man do not end here. In order to properly value the true worth of this man, one has to view his life against the backdrop of the history of the world as a whole. In this way we could have a greater appreciation of how this illiterate dweller of the Arabian Desert, who was born in the 'dark ages' some 1400 years ago, was the real pioneer of the modern age and the true leader of humanity. He is not only the leader of those who accept his leadership, but also of those who don't claim him as such- even of those who denounce him! The only difference being that the people who reject him are unaware of the fact that his guidance is still imperceptibly influencing their thoughts and their actions and is the governing principle of their lives and the very spirit of the modern age.

He was the one who turned the trend of human thought away from superstition, fear of the unknown and illogical religious demands, towards a more rational approach based on the love for truth, and a pious, balanced worldly life. He was the one who lived in a world in which miracles were demanded as a kind of supernatural 'sign' of a leader's divine favor, and yet he inspired in them the desire to look for rational proof and to hold that up as the standard for evidence.

He was the one who opened the eyes of those who had always been accustomed until then to look for messages from God in the weather or in natural occurrences. He was the one who, in place of unfounded speculation, led human beings to the path of rational understanding and sound reasoning on the basis of observation, experiment, and research. He was the one who clearly defined the limits and functions of sensory perception, reason, and intuition. He was the one who brought about a truce between spiritual and material values. He was the one who harmonized faith with reason and action. He was the one who created the basis for the scientific spirit, and infused it with the power of religion, and who evolved true religiosity on the basis of the scientific method.

## Some Gifts from Islamic Civilization

1. Science. There was never a conflict between religion and science in Muslim history. That is because the guiding principle of the Qur'an is that scientific inquiry leads to a greater understanding of God's power and creativity. The entire body of modern science is built upon the discoveries of Muslim researchers during what is termed as the Golden Age of Islam (9th through the 13th centuries). Muslims refined existing mathematics and invented new principles resulting in such arts as algebra and advanced geometry. They were the first to systematically study the inner workings of the body's organs, blood and major systems resulting in the most advanced medical encyclopedias in the world. They made important discoveries in chemistry, botany and geography, and also optical sciences.

2. Economics. Muslim merchants introduced to the Europeans the idea of banking institutions that would honor checks written by banks in far away locations. Curbs on debt exploitation, which are a hallmark of Islamic social justice, also influenced European thinkers.

3. Everyday life. Westerners would be surprised at how many features, products and discoveries from Muslim civilization still touch upon their lives today. Here is a sample of just a few of the 10,000 words of Arabic origin that are in the English language today: Admiral, Alcohol, Almanac, Candy, Check, Cotton, Guitar, Sofa, Zero, Tariff, Chemistry, Algebra, Algorithm, Aloe, Lemon, Mascara, Sugar, Giraffe, Magazine and Horizon.

Muhammad was the one who stamped out idolatry, the worship of man-gods and also polytheism in all its forms so thoroughly, and created such a firm faith in the unitary nature of God, that even those religions which were based entirely on superstitions and idolatry were compelled to adopt a monotheistic framework. He was the one who changed the basic concepts of ethics and spirituality.

To those who believed that asceticism and self-annihilation alone formed the standard of moral and spiritual purity, believing that purity could only be achieved by running away from worldly life, disregarding all the urges of the flesh and subjecting the body to all sorts of discomfort, he was the one who showed them how to negotiate the path to spiritual evolution, moral emancipation, and the attainment of salvation through an active participation in the practical affairs of the world around them.

He was the one who brought home to all of us our true worth and status. Those who believe in a god born on earth or in a son of a god as their theological foundation were told that human beings like themselves, who have no pretensions about being part of God, can become the representative of God on earth. Those who proclaim that powerful kings are their gods were made to understand that their false lords were merely humans like themselves and nothing more.

He was the one who stressed the principle that no person could claim holiness, authority, or kingship as their birthright, and that no one was born with the stigma of untouchability, slavery, or being of a lower class on their person. It was he and his teaching which inspired the idea of the unity of humanity, the equality of all human beings, true democracy and real freedom in the world.

"All of you belong to the line of Adam and Adam was created from dust. An Arab is not better than a non-Arab, nor is a white better than a black."

-Prophet Muhammad, peace be upon him

Leaving aside this line of thought and moving on a bit one can find countless practical results of the leadership of this illiterate man firmly impressed upon the laws and ways of the world. So many principles of good behavior, culture and civilization, purity of thought and deed, which are prevalent in the world today, owe their origin to him.

The social laws which he imparted have infiltrated deep into the structure of human social life, and this process continues up to this very day. The basic principles of economics which he taught have ushered in many a movement in world history and hold out the same promise for the future. The laws of governance which he formulated brought about many an upheaval in the political notions and theories of the world and continue to assert their influence even today.

The fundamental principles of law and justice, which bear the stamp of his genius, have influenced to a remarkable degree the administration of justice in the courts of nations, and form a perpetual source of guidance for all legal scholars to come. This illiterate Arab was the first person to set on a solid footing practically the whole framework of international relations, and regulated the basic foundation of the laws of war and peace. For no one had previously even the remotest idea that there could be an ethical code of war or that relations between different nations could be regulated on the grounds of common humanity.

## The Revolution Begins

In the panorama of world history the noble example of Muhammad, peace be upon him, towers high above many of the great leaders that have arisen through the ages, even of those famous people who are held up as the very lifeblood of their nations. The achievements of many of these 'heroes' oftentimes appear inadequate when contrasted with his life and work. Few of them possessed the ability to make such a long lasting change upon human civilization that would survive much beyond their own lifespan, rather, their efforts often touched upon no more than one or two facets of human interest. Some invented new theories and ideas, but were unable to turn their discoveries into practical reality.

Others were actively engaged in producing results, but they would often be held back by their lack of a truly depthful education. Some were renowned as statesmen only; others as masters of strategy and maneuvering. Some concentrated on one aspect of social improvement while unconsciously leaving many other sectors of need overlooked. Some have devoted their lives to discovering ethical and spiritual truths, only to ignore economics and politics. Others advanced economics and politics, but neglected morals and the spiritual side of life. As you can see, it is more often the case with great heroes, scientists and leaders that their talent is usually confined to a narrow agenda and rarely strays into expansive and comprehensive change such as would alter the course of human civilization for all times to come.

Muhammad, peace be upon him, is the only comprehensive example in which all the best qualities of a leader, reformer, thinker and activist have been blended together into one personality. He was a philosopher and a prophet and also the living embodiment of his own teachings. He was a great statesman as well as a military genius. He was a legislator and also a teacher of morals. He was a spiritual luminary as well as a religious guide. His vision penetrated every aspect of life and there was nothing that he didn't touch upon and improve. His teachings and advice covered a vast field of both personal and social reforms from the regulation of international relations down to the habits of everyday life like how to eat and drink with good manners, and even cleanse the body properly.

Set firmly upon the foundation of his beliefs, he established a civilization and a culture and produced such a fine balance among the conflicting aspects of life that there is not to be found even the slightest trace of any flaw, deficiency, or incompleteness. Can anyone from any other example boast of such a complete and all around sense of vision?

Most of the famous personalities of the world are said to be the products of their environment, but his case is unique. His environment seems to have played almost no part in the making of his personality. There is nothing in Arabian society or history at that time to explain the rise of such a unique and unexpected man. At the most all that can be said is that the lawless and divided loyalties prevalent in Arabia at that time cried out for the appearance of such a person who could knit together the warring tribes into one nation: someone who could lay the foundation for their economic integration and success which would enable them to bring the nations around them under heel.

In short, the only thing that that barren land needed was a national leader who would have all the traits of an Arab chieftain and, through cruelty, oppression, bloodshed, deceit, and hypocrisy, or by any other fair or foul means, could have enriched his own people, and left a kingdom as a heritage for his successors. One cannot prove that Arabia needed anything more than that kind of leader, much less a spiritual visionary.

If we look at Hegel's philosophy of history or at Karl Marx's theories of historical materialism, again, we could only conclude that the time and environment in Arabia in the sixth century demanded only the emergence of a leader who could create a unified nation and build up an empire.

But Hegelian or Marxist philosophy cannot explain how such an environment could produce a man whose mission was to teach the best morals, to purify humanity of all bad habits, and to wipe out prejudices and superstitions that were holdovers from the days of ignorance and darkness, who looked beyond the watertight compartments of race, nation, and country, who laid the foundations of a moral, spiritual, cultural and political superstructure for the good of the world and not for his country alone, who practically, not theoretically, placed business transactions, civics, politics, and international relations on moral grounds and produced such a balanced and temperate synthesis between worldly life and spiritual advancement that even to this day it is considered a masterpiece of wisdom and foresight exactly in the same way as it was considered in his lifetime. Can anyone honestly say that such a person was the product of backward and uncivilized Arabia?

He doesn't only appear to be independent of his environment, rather, when we look at his achievements we are irresistibly drawn to the conclusion that he actually transcends all limitation of time and space. His vision broke through all temporal and physical barriers, passed beyond centuries and millenniums and comprehended within itself the entirety of human activity and the whole of human history. He is not one of those whom history has cast into a dustbin, and he is not praised only because he was just a good leader in his own time. He is that unique and incomparable leader of humanity who marches with the time, who is modern in every age and in every era, even as he was in his own moment of history. Truly, his teachings are as modern today as they were yesterday.

Famous personalities that are labeled 'makers of history' are often only 'subjects of history'. Muhammad, peace be upon him, is in fact, taking into account the entire width and breadth of history, a unique example of a true 'maker of history'. If we study the lives and circumstances of the great leaders of the world who brought about great changes and even revolutions in thought, we often find that, even before their involvement, the forces of revolution were already gathering momentum for the destined upheaval.

Trends were taking their course and moving society in certain directions and were only waiting for the right moment to burst out. In harnessing these gathering forces for action, most revolutionary leaders played the part of an actor for whom the stage and the role had already been set beforehand.

On the other hand, amidst all the many 'makers of history' and revolutionary figures through the ages, Muhammad, peace be upon him, was the only person who had to find the ways and the means to bring together the wherewithal of revolution, who had to mold and produce the kind of men and women he wanted for his purpose because the very spirit of revolution and its required ingredients were nonexistent in those people among whom his lot was cast.

## The Witness of Historians

"Philosopher, orator, apostle, legislator, warrior, conqueror of ideas, restorer of rational dogmas, of a cult without images; the founder of twenty terrestrial empires and of one spiritual empire, that is Muhammad. As regards all standards by which human greatness may be measured, we may well ask, is there a man greater than he?"

- Lamartine, Historie de la Turquie, vol. II, pp. 276-277

"My choice of Muhammad to lead the list of the world's most influential persons may surprise some readers and may be questioned by others, but he was the only man in history who was supremely successful on both the religious and secular level."

- Michael H. Hart, The 100: A Ranking of the Most Influential Persons in History, New York: Hart Publishing Co., Inc., 1978, p. 33

Think about it: he made a profound impression upon the hearts and minds of thousands of his disciples strictly through the sheer force of his personality and molded them according to his need. Through his iron will he, himself, prepared the ground for revolution, molded its shape and features, and directed the resultant currents and trends into a single, irresistible channel, all of his own accord. Can anyone cite another example of a maker of history of such brilliance and splendor?

## The Last Word

We may ponder over this matter and wonder how it was possible that 1,400 years ago, in a backward region of the earth like Arabia, an illiterate Arab trader and herdsman came to possess such light, such knowledge, such power, such capabilities, and such finely-developed moral virtues that he could transform a culture, establish a religion and lay the groundwork for a civilization that has come to include over a billion followers worldwide and stretch in a band around the earth from Suriname, South America to Indonesia, in Asia.

One could say that there is nothing special about his message, that it was just the product of his own mind. But if that were the case, why stop at just being a prophet? He should have proclaimed himself to be a god, or the son of god! If he would have made such a claim at that time, the nations of the earth, who already had no hesitation in calling Krishna and Buddha as gods and Jesus a son of God, and who even worshipped the forces of nature like fire, water and air, would have readily accepted such a wonderful person as the Lord God Himself!

But look! His assertion is just to the contrary. For he proclaimed this message about himself: To paraphrase he said, "I am a human being like yourselves. I have not brought any thing to you of my own accord. All of it has been revealed to me by God. Whatever I possess belongs to Him. This message, which no one can duplicate with their own talent, is not from my own mind. Every word of it has been sent down by God and all glory belongs to Him Whose Message it is. All the wonderful achievements which stand to my credit in your eyes, all the laws which I have given, all the principles which I have enumerated and taught- none of them is from me. I am not skilled enough to produce such work from my own personal ability and talent. I look to Divine Guidance in all matters. Whatever God wills I do; whatever He directs, I proclaim."

Listen to that! What a wonderful and inspiring example of honesty, truth, and honor it is! A liar or a hypocrite generally tries to take for himself all the credit for the deeds of others, even when the falsity of his statements can easily be proven. But this great man does not take any credit for any of these achievements, even when no one could contradict him, as there was no method for finding out the source of his inspiration.

What more proof of perfect honesty of purpose, uprightness of character, and nobility of soul can there be! Who else can be a more truthful person than the one who received such unique gifts and embellishments through an unidentifiable method, and yet still he clearly points out the source of all his enlightenment and inspiration? All these factors lead to the irresistible conclusion that such a man was the true Messenger of God.

Such was our Holy Prophet Muhammad (peace be upon him). He was a prodigy of extraordinary merits, a paragon of virtue and goodness, a symbol of truth and veracity, a great prophet of God and His Messenger to the entire world. His life and thought, his truth and straightforwardness, his piety and goodness, his character and morals, his ideology and achievements- all stand as unimpeachable proofs of his prophethood. Any human being who studies his life and teachings, without preconceived bias, will testify that he was indeed a true prophet of God and that the Qur'an- the Book he gave to humanity- is the Book of God. No unbiased and serious seeker after truth can escape this conclusion.

Furthermore, it must also be clearly understood that, now, only through Muhammad, peace be upon him, can we know the straight path of Islam. The Qur'an and Muhammad's life example are the only reliable sources that are available to humanity to learn God's Will in its entirety. Muhammad, peace be upon him, is the Messenger of God for the whole of the world and the long chain of prophets has come to an end with him. He was the last of the prophets and all the instructions which it was God's will to impart to mankind through direct revelation were sent by Him through Muhammad (peace be upon him) and are enshrined in the Qur'an and the Sunnah, or example of the Prophet.

Now, whoever is a seeker of truth and is anxious to become an honest Muslim and sincere follower of the straight way to God, must have faith in God's last prophet, accept his teachings and follow the way he pointed out to humanity. This is the road to success and eternal salvation.

## There will be no more Prophets

This brings us to the question of the finality of prophethood. We have already discussed the nature of prophethood and this discussion makes it clear that the appearance of a prophet is not an everyday occurrence. Nor is the physical presence of the prophet essential for every land, people, and time period. The life and teachings of the prophet are the beacon-light to guide a nation to the right path, and as long as his teachings and his guidance survive, he is, in a manner of speaking, still alive.

The real death of a prophet consists not in his physical demise but in the loss of his teachings and the alteration of his guidance. The earlier prophets then have all died in the sense that their followers have allowed their teachings to be corrupted, have altered their instructions, and have polluted their biographies by attaching fictitious events to them.

Not one of the earlier revelations- the Torah, the Psalms, the Gospel of Jesus, etc- exists today in its original text, and even the followers of these books confess that they do not possess the original and authentic books. The biographies of the earlier prophets have been so mixed up with fiction that an accurate and authentic understanding of their lives has become impossible. Accounts of their lives have been filled with tales and legends and no trustworthy record is a available anywhere. Not only have their records been lost and their life's work forgotten, but it can't even be said with certainty when and where any given prophet was born and raised, how he lived and what code he gave to his people. To reiterate, then, the real death of a prophet consists in the death of his teachings.

Judging the facts by this standard no one can deny that Muhammad, peace be upon him, and his teachings are alive. His teachings stand uncorrupted and are incorruptible. The Qur'an- the book he brought to the world- exists in its original text, without the slightest alteration of letter, syllable, order, or title. The entire account of his life- his sayings, instructions and actions- is preserved with startling accuracy, that even after the passage of fourteen centuries the history is so clear and complete that it seems as if we are seeing him with our own eyes.

No other human being's biography is so well preserved as that of Muhammad, the prophet of Islam (peace be upon him). In each and every matter of life we can seek the guidance of Muhammad, peace be upon him, and take a lesson from his life-example. That is why there is no need for any other prophet after him. A new prophet doesn't need to be sent just because one happens to pass away. If his teachings survive, then he is still alive. There are three conditions which are required for the raising of a new prophet. These may be summed up as follows:

1. If the teachings of the earlier prophets have been added to or corrupted or they have died and a revival of spiritual truth is needed, then God may send a new prophet. In such a case one is raised so that he can purge the impurities from the lives of his people and restore religion to its pristine form and purity.

2. If the teachings of a prophet who has passed away were incomplete and it is necessary to amend, add to or improve them, then a new prophet is sent to effect these changes.

3. If an earlier prophet was raised exclusively for a certain nation or region and a prophet for another nation, people, or country is required, then one will be chosen who can communicate in that other peoples' unique style and through their culture.

These are the three fundamental conditions which necessitate the raising of a new prophet. A careful perusal of the facts shows that none of these conditions exists today. The teachings of the last prophet, Muhammad, peace be upon him, are alive, have been fully preserved, and thus have been made immortal. The guidance he has shown to humanity is complete and flawless, and is enshrined in the Holy Qur'an. All the sources of Islam are fully intact and each and every instruction or action of the Holy Prophet can be ascertained without the least shadow of doubt. And so, because his teachings are fully intact, there is no need for any new prophet to be sent to the world.

Secondly, God has completed His revealed guidance through Prophet Muhammad, peace be upon him, and the religion known as Islam is the most complete way of life for humanity. God said just that in the Qur'an with these words: "Today I have perfected your way of life for you, and have completed My favor upon you and have chosen submission (to Me) as your way of life," and a thorough survey of just how Islam is a complete way of life will prove the truth of these Qur'anic words. Islam gives guidance for life in this world as well as the means to aid our journey into the hereafter. Nothing essential for living rightly has been left out. This system of life has now been perfected and there is no need for any other prophets to improve upon it.

Lastly, the Message of Muhammad, peace be upon him, was not meant for any particular people, place, or time. He was raised as a prophet for the entire world- the messenger of truth for all humanity. The Qur'an, which is God's revelation, directs Muhammad, peace be upon him, to say: "O humanity, I am God's Messenger to all of you." He has been described as "a blessing for all the people of the universe" and his approach has indeed been universal and humane. Again, that is why there remains no need for a new prophet after him. The Qur'an even labeled him as the Seal of Prophethood. So there you have it: the only source for knowing God accurately, and how to live in a way pleasing to Him, is Muhammad, peace be upon him.

We can only know how to truly submit to God through his teachings, which are so complete and so comprehensive that the world does not need any new prophet; it only needs people who have full faith in Muhammad (peace be upon him), and who will become the standard-bearers of his message, propagate it to the world at large, and endeavor to establish the culture which Muhammad (peace be upon him) gave to humanity. The world needs people who can translate his teachings into practice and establish a society which is governed by Divine Law. It needs people who will work to make this kind of society a reality: the society of God, whose supremacy Muhammad (peace be upon him) came to establish. This is the mission of Muhammad, peace be upon him, and the success of the world depends on the success of his mission.

# 4

# What Does Islam Teach?

Before we go any further, let's review what we've learned thus far and sum up the essence of what Islam is all about. A concise summary is as follows:

Islam means submission and obedience to God, the Lord of the Universe. The only authentic and reliable source for knowing about God, His Will and His Law are through the teachings of a true prophet. Therefore, we can define Islam as a religion that stands for complete faith in the teachings of the prophet and an unflinching obedience to his way of life. Consequently, whoever ignores the example of the prophet and claims to follow God directly is not really 'surrendered' to God at all.

In ancient times there were always separate prophets for separate nations. The history of prophethood shows that in some especially critical times several prophets were commissioned in succession for a single nation. In ancient days, Islam was not the official name of the spiritual paths that were imparted to those nations by their prophets, though the messages always contained the core principle of what Islam represents. The basic foundations of God's universal religion were the same in every age and country, it was only the forms of worship, the codes of law, and other detailed rules and regulations for godly living that were different, according to the local culture and particular conditions of each people. It was not necessary for one nation to follow another nation's prophet and its responsibility was confined only to following the guidance given to it by its own prophet.

The age of recurring prophethood came to an end with the advent of Muhammad, peace be upon him. The teachings of Islam (submission to God) were made complete through him. Now there could be one basic law formulated for the needs of the entire world. Muhammad, peace be upon him, was designed to be the prophet for all of humanity. His prophetic mission was not meant for any individual nation or country or time; his message was meant for all peoples and for all ages. With his appearance, all earlier spiritual paths were made obsolete. Muhammad, peace be upon him, brought to the world a complete code of life.

So from then on, no other prophet would be sent to the world and no other Divinely sanctioned way of life would be born until the end of time. Muhammad's teachings, peace be upon him, are meant for all the children of Adam- the entire human race! True submission to God would forever after consist of following Muhammad, acknowledging his prophethood, believing in all that he asked us to believe in, following him in both letter and spirit, and submitting to all of his commands and injunctions as the very embodiment of the Will of God. This is submission to God; this is Islam.

This final point naturally brings us to ask the question: What did Muhammad, peace be upon him, ask us to believe in? What are the major points of doctrine in Islam? We have now reached the point where we can explore these doctrines fully. And as you read about the teachings of Islam you may come to find that not only are they simple, honest, endearing and valuable, but they are also an essential means for humanity to bring out the best in itself both in this life and in the life to come.

## God is One: Islam and Monotheism

The most important teaching of Prophet Muhammad, peace be upon him, is to believe in the oneness of God. This concept is expressed in the primary statement of faith known as the *Kalima*, or Primary Phrase. In Arabic it goes like this: *La elaha ill Allah* "There is no god but the God". This beautiful phrase is the bedrock of Islam, its foundation and its essence. It is the expression of this belief which distinguishes a true Muslim from a kafir (a concealer of God's truth), an idolater, or an atheist. The acceptance or denial of this one phrase produces a world of difference between one person and another.

Those who hold it to be true become members of a united community, while those who don't believe in it form a block of opposition. For the believers there is unbridled progress and eventual success in this world as well as the ultimate success in the hereafter, while failure and shamefulness are the ultimate fate of those who refuse to believe in it.

But the difference which occurs between the believers and the unbelievers is not the result of the mere chanting of a few words. Obviously, just saying a phrase or two cannot bring about such a tremendous division. The real force and power lies in the conscious acceptance of this doctrine along with its stipulations and finally the complete adherence to its dictates in daily life. Unless you know the real meaning implicit in the phrase "there is no god but the God" and its importance in guiding human life, you cannot realize the true significance of this doctrine.

---

### An Important Question

*If Islam teaches that God has no gender, then why does the Qur'an call 'Allah' a 'He'? There is no term for 'It' in the Arabic language. All words are assigned a gender, male or female. The same is true of Spanish and other languages. So while 'mesa' means 'table' in Spanish, it is called a feminine word and gets the feminine article ("la=the") which causes us to say, 'la mesa'. It doesn't mean a table is a 'girl.' As opposed to 'el camino' or 'the road' which doesn't mean that a road is a 'boy' just because the masculine 'el' article is used. ("el=the" in Spanish also)*

Arabic works exactly the same way. What is interesting is that the name 'Allah' comes the closest to being a gender neutral word in Arabic from the fact that the masculine article 'hua' (He, it) is used while the last two letters of the name 'Allah' (the ah sound) is a feminine ending. So saying 'Hua Allah' (He is Allah) with a masculine article and a feminine ending essentially cancels each gender out.

The thrust of the doctrine would never become effective unless these essentials are achieved. Chanting the word 'food' over and over won't make hunger go away; saying the name of a medicine a thousand times won't heal the disease. In the same way, if the *Kalima* is repeated endlessly, without any understanding of its meaning and implications, it won't produce the revolution which it is meant to bring about.

The revolution in thought and society can occur only if a person grasps the full meaning of this doctrine, realizes its significance, places true faith in it, and accepts and follows it in letter as well as spirit. Unless the understanding of the doctrine of God's unity is developed it cannot become fully effective. We avoid fire because we know that it burns; we keep away from poison because we believe that it can kill. Similarly, if the real significance of pure Monotheism is fully grasped, it should necessarily make us avoid, in belief as well as in action, every form and shade of disbelief, atheism, and polytheism. This is the natural dictate of belief in the Unity of God.

## What does this Mean?

In the Arabic language the word *elah* means 'someone or something that is worshipped'. In other words, an *elah* is a being who is so great and powerful that it must be held in awe, bowed to in humility and approached in submission. Generally, then, *elah* is translated into English as a god, and is related to the Hebrew word, *eloh*. In addition, an *elah* can be any being who possesses power too great to be comprehended by humans.

The definition of a god also includes their possessing unlimited power- power that is so spectacular that it can astonish others. It also conveys the sense that others are dependent upon that god and that he (or it) is not dependent upon anyone else. The word *elah* also carries a sense of concealment and mystery, that is, any god worth his salt should be unseen and imperceptible, not strutting around in the street or hanging in the sky in search of attention. The word *dios* in Spanish, *khuda* in Farsi, and god in English bear, more or less, the same meaning. Other languages of the world also contain words with a similar import.

There is another word in Arabic, however, that is greater than the term for a mere god. That word is Allah, and it is the personal name of God. It is the only word in Arabic that has no specific male or female connotation, it cannot be made plural and there is no diminutive form such as saying demi-god in English. The *Kalima*, that we discussed before, expresses this concept in its fullest sense and literally means: "There is no god other than the One Great Being known as the One and Only God."

This tells us that in the whole of the universe, there is absolutely no one else worthy to be worshipped other than the one true God, that heads should bow only to Him, that only He possesses all power, that all are in need of His favor, and that all are obliged to seek His help. He is hidden from our five physical senses, and our intellect fails to perceive what He is. Now that we know what the primary doctrine of Islam is, let's take a look at how this teaching influences the life of the world.

From the earliest written records of our kind, as well as from the oldest relics of antiquity that archaeologists have been able to discover, it seems evident that in every age people have believed in some kind of a god or gods and have worshipped them profusely. Even in our own times every nation on the face of the earth, from the most primitive to the most advanced, believes in and worships some kind of supernatural being. This shows that the idea of having a god and of worshipping him (or it) is ingrained in human nature. The latest scientific research even suggests that we are 'hard-wired' with a 'god-gene' within our very genetic code that causes us to seek a power greater than ourselves.

But this begs the question: What is that impulse all about? Where does it arise, and why do people feel so compelled to act upon it? We can deduce the answer to this question if we just take a moment to consider the place of humanity in this wide universe. A closer look into our selves and our nature from this vantage point shows that we are not omnipotent. Neither are we self-sufficient and self-existing, nor are our powers without limitation.

In fact, we are weak, frail, needy, and destitute. We are dependent upon a multitude of forces and without their assistance we cannot make any headway. There are countless things necessary to maintain our existence such as healthy food, clean water and a stable environment, but none of them are completely and totally within our power. Sometimes they come into our possession in a direct and systematic way, and at times we find ourselves deprived of them.

But even beyond the basic necessities of life, there are a lot of precious and important things that we try to arrange for such as safety for our families, investments for the future, wealth and increased opportunity. Sometimes we are successful and other times we aren't. That's because it's not completely within our own power to gain these things. There are a lot of factors out there that are working against our success. We take a chance, but the hand of fate sometimes brings our hopes to a sudden end.

Disease, stress, sickness, miscalculation and unforeseen variables always threaten us and seem poised to sabotage our path to happiness. And even while we work overtime to try and avoid these kinds of problems and setbacks, we may end up achieving both success and failure at the same time! Even if it seems, one day, that we have reached the pinnacle of our desires, fortune may strike us down again through disaster or disease or any number of things. Then what do we have?

Turning to the wide, wide world around us, there are so many things whose immensity and scale impress us, making us feel truly insignificant and puny. Think of towering mountains and thundering waterfalls, gigantic animals and ferocious beasts of prey. We may experience earthquakes, hurricanes, floods and other natural disasters. We look skyward and see the clouds over our heads and feel a sense of foreboding when they become thick and dark. Peals of thunder, flashes of lightning and continuous downpours of heavy rain bring us to a momentary realization about our fragility. We see the sun, the moon, and the stars in their constant motion. We reflect upon how great, powerful, and grand these bodies are, and, in contrast to them, how frail and tiny we, ourselves, are!

The assurance that the sun will always come up tomorrow betrays the belief inherent in all of us that there is a reliable order to the universe and how it functions.

The vast phenomena all around us, and the consciousness of our own weakness, impress upon us a deep sense of our own unimportance, smallness, and helplessness. Isn't it natural, then, that we begin to see the hand of a Greater Power behind all that is, especially since we, alone, out of all other creatures, seem to be capable of making such a leap of understanding to begin with? Indeed, we begin to think of that Force which can wield such great power. The sense of its utter strength makes us long to seek its aid in such a precarious world of existence. We might even get to the point where we want to do whatever it takes to please that Power so that we might receive some favorable notice, and we may feel a sense of dread at stirring up the displeasure of that Power lest we may be destroyed by it.

In the most primitive stage of religious development, people have thought that the great objects of nature, whose grandeur and glory are visible before their eyes, and which appear to be harmful or beneficial to him, hold in themselves the real power and authority, and therefore, are divine. Thus people have worshipped trees, lions, birds, stars, the sun, volcanoes, clouds and numerous other objects. This is the lowest form of religious misunderstanding.

When humanity's ignorance dissipated to some extent, and a few glimmers of light and knowledge began to appear on its intellectual horizon, people came to the realization that these great and powerful objects were, in themselves, quite mechanical and dependent upon nature, and were no better in status than people-rather they were of a lower degree in value! The largest and the strongest animal dies just like the tiniest germ, and loses all its ferocity; great rivers rise and fall and then one day wind up as dry river beds; the high mountains are blasted and shattered by humanity itself; the productiveness of the earth is not even under the earth's own control- for water is what makes any given region prosperous, while a lack of water makes any place barren overnight.

Even rain is not able to control itself. It depends upon air currents and evaporation to make clouds and then only falls when the atmospheric conditions allow it. The atmosphere, too, is powerless to effect any change and its usefulness depends upon the many gasses that are fed into it from the respiration of plant life, sun light and other factors. The sun, the moon, and the stars also are bound up by a powerful law outside whose dictates they cannot make the slightest movement.

After these considerations, the collective mind of humanity turned to the possibility that some great mysterious power of a divine nature controlled the objects it saw and was the real source of authority in the universe. But these reflections soon gave rise to the erroneous idea that there were individual powers behind the various components of nature. Polytheism was soon to follow. This belief system holds that there are countless "mini-gods" who are supposed to be in charge of their own departments in nature, such as a wind god, sun god, water god, hunting god, harvest god, and on and on and on. In time elaborate idols were erected and art was created to venerate them in society. And thus people began to worship those statues and works of art. All of this was just another form of religious misunderstanding. The unvarnished truth remained hidden from human eyes even at this stage of intellectual and cultural development.

As human civilization progressed even further in knowledge and understanding, and as great minds reflected more and more deeply upon the fundamental problems of life and existence, many came to realize that there was more to nature than just a collection of competing gods. They understood that there was some kind of a unified principle and power at work in the universe. They noted that there was a consistent regularity to every sunrise and sunset, and that there was a curious kind of logic in the seasonal operation of the winds and rains, in the motion of the stars and even in the change of the seasons.

They saw countless different forces working together, in a wonderfully harmonious way, and were stunned by what they saw as a highly potent and ultimately well-thought out system operating in nature. So many divergent paths all weaving together to produce gravity, seasonal cycles, motion, weather, climate, and even- life- as if it were all meant to work together to produce some kind of predetermined result!

Observing this uniformity, this regularity, and this complete obedience to a unified code in nature, even a person who believes in many gods finds himself obliged to believe that there must be one force that is greater than all the others, who exercises supreme authority over all. For, if there were separate, equal gods, the whole machinery of the universe would be in constant imbalance as each god tries to increase his power in relation to the rest.

Human beings have called this greatest of deities by different names, such as 'God,' 'Dios,' 'Allah,' 'the Great Spirit,' etc., but because the darkness of ignorance still persisted in the minds of many, countless misguided souls still continued to worship lesser false gods, right alongside the Supreme One.

Many societies have imagined that the Divine Kingdom of God was not much different than earthly kingdoms. Just as a ruler has many ministers, trusted associates, governors, and other responsible officials, so too, they reasoned, the minor gods were likewise merely helpers of a sort. The Great Overlord, they assumed, could not be approached without pleasing and placating the officials under Him. So they must also be worshipped and appealed to for help, and should in no wise be offended. And so the idols were regarded as God's assistants through whom we must present our appeal to the Lord.

The more humanity increased in knowledge, however, the greater became its dissatisfaction with the crowded field of gods to worship. So over time the number of minor deities began to decrease. More enlightened thinkers brought each one of them under the searchlight of scrutiny and ultimately found that none of those man-made deities had any real power; they themselves were created concepts from someone's mind, just figments of an ancient active imagination. They were thus dropped one by one until the acceptance of only one God remained.

The ancient Hebrews were among the first to actively champion this cause, followed by the Christians later on, yet the concept of the one true God was inevitably contaminated by persistent elements from the days of polytheistic ignorance. Many people now image that God looks just like a man, as if He were one of us, or that we are modeled after His physical characteristics. They even say that He prefers one ethnic group among humanity more than others. Some believe that God, Himself, came down to the earth in human form- first as a baby in a crib and then growing up into manhood.

Others think that God got tired from creating the universe and had to take a day off to rest. Some believe that it's necessary to approach God through the help of saints and spirits, and that nothing can be achieved without their intercession. Some imagine God to have a certain form or image, and they believe it's necessary to keep paintings and statues before them for the purposes of worship. Such distorted notions of the Divine One have persisted and lingered, and many of them are prevalent among different people even until this very day.

Islam has another approach to conceptualizing God, and it is embodied in the Arabic word, *Tawheed*. This term literally means Unity, Uniqueness and Oneness. In other words, it means monotheism, the belief in one God. Monotheism is the highest form of theology, and it is precisely this knowledge that God has sent to humanity in all ages through His prophets. It was this knowledge that was revealed to Adam, Noah, Abraham, Moses and Jesus, God's blessings be upon them all! And it was this very knowledge that Muhammad, God's blessings be upon him, brought to humanity anew. It is true knowledge, pure and absolute, without the least shade of ignorance.

The greater part of humanity is guilty of polytheism, idolatry and *kufr* only because it turned away from the teachings of the prophets and depended upon its own faulty reasoning, false perceptions or biased interpretations. Monotheism dispels all the clouds of ignorance and illuminates the horizon with the light of reality. Now let's examine the plain truth that this concept of monotheism, as contained in the short phrase, "There is no god but the God," points us towards, what truth it conveys and what kind of belief systems it fosters. This we can grasp if we ponder over the following points.

The first question to tackle is the nature of the one who is in control of this universe. Every day we come face to face with a grand, limitless universe. Our minds fail to comprehend the utter depth of its beginning nor can we properly visualize its end. It has been moving on in its charted course from time immemorial and will continue its journey into the vast vista of the future long after we are gone. Creatures beyond number have appeared in it- and go on appearing every day. The signs are so bewildering that a thinking mind finds itself aghast and wonderstruck. We are unable to fully understand and grasp the reality of its immensity solely through our own puny vision. We can't bring ourselves to believe that all of this just appeared one day by random chance or accident.

The universe is not some lucky mass of atoms that just got the combination right. It's not just a jumble of uncoordinated objects. It is not a conglomeration of things both chaotic and meaningless. All of this that we see can't be without some kind of a Creator, a Designer, a Controller, a Governor.

Who can create and control this majestic universe? Only a being who is completely powerful, all wise, omnipotent and omniscient- who is all-knowing and all-seeing. He must have supreme authority over all that exists in the universe. He must possess limitless powers, must be the lord of the universe and all that it contains, and He must be free from every flaw and weakness. No one should have the power to interfere with His work. Only a being like that can be the Creator, the Controller and the Governor of the Universe.

Secondly, it is essential that all these divine attributes and powers must be vested into one being- it is virtually impossible for two or more distinct personalities to have similar powers equally co-existing. They are bound to collide with each other eventually. Logic dictates that there must be one- and only one- Supreme Being Who has control over all other beings. You would never accept that there would be two governors for the same state or two supreme generals for the same army!

Similarly, the idea that different 'gods' would have different powers or departments, for instance, that one of them has all knowledge, the other all fortune and still another all life-giving abilities, is ludicrous. The universe is an indivisible whole and each one of those 'gods' would inevitably be dependent upon the others on some level. If that were the case, the universe could easily fall to pieces if there was only one small slip up on the part of one 'god' or another.

To continue under the odd assumption that several gods or distinct persons of a godhead exist in an otherwise unified universe, then, we must also take the position that the attributes of the god or gods in question must be non-transferable. It wouldn't be possible that a certain quality in a certain deity would suddenly disappear and be found in another deity. For example, a divine being who can't save himself from death surely can't give life to others. The one who can't protect his own divine self is definitely unsuited to govern the vast limitless universe.

And so the longer you reflect upon the problem, the firmer your conviction will be that all these divine powers and attributes must exist in one and the same

Being exclusively. Thus polytheism is really baseless and cannot stand up to rational scrutiny. It is simply an impractical possibility. The facts of life and nature do not fit into that kind of belief system. All the signposts all around us automatically bring us to the stark reality that strict and pure monotheism is the only logical and real option.

Now, keeping in mind this logical and clean cut conception of God, cast a searching glance at this vast universe. Exert yourself to the utmost and see if you can find among all the objects that you observe, among all the things that you perceive, among all that you can think, feel, or imagine- all that your knowledge can comprehend- anyone possessing these attributes. The sun, the moon, the stars, animals, birds, fish, even atoms, or any person or group of people- do any of them possess these attributes? Certainly not! For everything in the universe is created, is controlled and regulated, is dependent upon others, is mortal and transitory, is not self-acting and self-propelling- its slightest movements are controlled by an irresistible law and it cannot deviate from that law.

Their helpless condition proves that the cloak of divinity cannot fit their stature. They don't possess the slightest trace of divinity and have absolutely no relationship to it. They are simply without any godly powers and it is a travesty of truth and a folly of the highest magnitude to attribute to them divine status. This is the true significance of the opening words of the *Kalima*: '*La elaha*,' i.e. 'there is no god...' No human or material object possesses divine power and authority deserving of worship and obedience.

---

### The Qur'an on God:

"God! There is no god but He, the Living,
Who needs no other but Whom all others need.
He is never drowsy nor does He rest.
To Him belongs space and the Earth;
Who can intercede without His consent?

He knows everything people have done and will
do, and no one can grasp the least of His
knowledge, without His review.

His throne extends over space and the Earth and
He tires not in their safekeeping. He alone is
Most High, the Lord Sovereign Supreme."

- Chapter 2, verse 255

---

But this not the end of our quest. We have found that divinity does dwell in any material or human element of the universe, and that none of them possesses even the slightest trace of it. This very inquiry leads us to the conclusion that there is a Supreme Being, over and above all that our unwary eyes see in the universe, Who possesses all Divine attributes, Who is the Will behind all nature, the Creator of this grand universe, the Controller of its superb Law, the Governor of its serene

135

rhythm, the Administrator of all its working: He is Allah, the Lord of the Universe, and He has no associates in His Divinity. This is what the next part of the *Kalima* teaches us: 'ill Allah,' '...except the God.'

This knowledge is superior to all other kinds of knowledge and the greater you exert yourself in understanding it, the deeper will be your conviction that this is the starting point of all progress. In every field of study, whether it is physics, chemistry, astronomy, geology, biology, zoology, economics, politics, sociology, or the humanities, you will find that the deeper you probe, the clearer will become the indications of the truth of *La elaha ill Allah*. It is this concept which opens up the doors of knowledge with the light of reality. And if you deny or disregard this reality, you will find that at every step you will meet disillusionment and open-ended questions, for the denial of this primary truth robs everything in creation of its real meaning and true significance. The universe becomes somewhat meaningless and overly mechanized. The justification for progress itself will become blurred and confused.

## How does it Influence Humanity?

Now let us study the results of what belief in pure monotheism brings into the lives of each and every one of us, and then we can see why it can always be a source for success in our lives, both here and in the hereafter.

*Result #1*

A believer in this doctrine can never be narrow-minded or parochial in outlook. He believes in a God who is the Creator of the heavens and the earth, the Master of the East and the West and the Sustainer of the entire universe. After this realization is achieved he will never regard anything in the world as being strange. He will look upon everything in the universe as belonging to the same Lord whom he himself belongs to. He will not be partisan in his thinking and behavior. His sympathy, love, and service will not remain confined to any particular race or group. His vision will be enlarged, his intellectual horizon will widen, and his outlook will become liberal and as all encompassing as is the Kingdom of God. How can this expansive vision and open mindedness be achieved by an atheist, who believes in nothing but 'survival of the fittest', or by a polytheist, who thinks of only his own idol in a sea of idols, or by one who believes in a god who is no better than any of us in that he, too, walked around on earth, answered the call of nature and cried out in fear?

This belief produces in a person the highest degree of self-respect and self-esteem. The believer knows that God alone is the possessor of all power, and that no one besides Him can benefit or harm a person, or provide for his need, or give and take away life, or wield authority or influence.

This conviction makes him indifferent to, and independent and fearless of, all powers other than those of God. He never bows his head in homage to any of God's creatures, nor does he stretch his hand pleadingly before anyone else. And he is certainly not over impressed by anybody's greatness. This quality or attitude of mind cannot be produced by any other belief system. For it is necessary that those who associate other beings with God, or who deny God, should bow in homage to some creatures, regard them able to benefit or harm them, and repose all their hopes in them.

## Result #2

Along with self-respect, this belief also generates in a person a sense of modesty and humbleness. It makes him shy and unpretentious. A sincere believer is never proud, haughty or arrogant. The boisterous pride of power, wealth and status can have no room in his heart, because he knows that whatever he possesses has been given to him by God, and can be taken away by Him just as He can give.

In contrast to this, an unbeliever, when he achieves some worldly gain, becomes proud and conceited because he believes that his success is due to his own abilities. In the same way pride and self conceit are a necessary outcome and component of idolatry, because a person who thinks there are many personal gods believes that he has a particular relationship with 'his' god that no one else shares.

## Result #3

This belief makes a person virtuous and moral. He has the conviction that there is no other means of success and salvation for him except purity of soul and righteousness of behavior. He has perfect faith in God who is above all needs, is related to no one, is absolutely just, and that no one has any hand or influence in the exercise of His divine powers. This belief creates in him the consciousness that, unless he lives rightly and acts justly, he cannot succeed.

No call to influence or underhanded activity can save him from ruin. As against this, the truth-hiders and idolaters always live with false hopes. Some of them believe that God had a son who will atone for their sins; some think that they are God's favorites, and will not be punished; others believe that their saints will intercede with God on their behalf while still others believe that their deities can be bribed into accepting their immoral lives and frivolous deeds. As for atheists, they don't believe that there is any Being at all having power over them, to whom they would be responsible for their good or bad action; therefore they consider themselves altogether independent to act in whatever way they like in this world. Their own fancies become their gods and they live like slaves to their wishes and desires.

## *Result #4*

The believer does not become despondent and broken-hearted under any circumstances. He or she has firm faith in God, who is the Master of all the treasures of the heavens and the earth, whose grace and bounty have no limit and whose powers are infinite. This faith imparts to his heart extraordinary consolation, fills it with satisfaction and keeps it filled with hope. In this world he might meet with rejection from every door; maybe nothing in this life will ever seem to go right and all hope will seem to desert him. But faith in and dependence upon God never leave him; and on their strength he goes on struggling.

Such profound confidence can result from no other belief than belief in one God. Idolaters, truth-hiders, and atheists have weaker coping skills; they depend upon limited vistas of understanding; therefore in hours of trouble they are soon overwhelmed by despair and, frequently they succumb to substance abuse, mental conditions, self-destructive behavior, cynicism and some even commit suicide.

## Result #5

This belief in pure monotheism also produces in people a very strong degree of determination, patient perseverance, and trust in God. When a person makes up his mind and devotes his resources to fulfill Divine Commands in order to secure God's pleasure, he is sure he has the support and backing of the Lord of the universe. This certainty makes him firm and as strong as a mountain.

No amount of hardship, obstacles, or hostile opposition can make him give up his resolution. Someone who believes in many fickle gods, or who thinks that God is a partnership, or who doesn't believe in any divine presence at all cannot hope to develop this kind of rock-solid resolution. They will always be filled with doubts as to the ultimate worth of their purpose.

## Result #6

Pure monotheism, without any reservation or conflicting theories, inspires bravery in the believer. There are two things that make a person a coward:

1. Hating death while loving comfort.

2. The belief that we can ward off death if we can just pull off the right scheme, placate the right deity, get lucky or bribe someone.

Believing that there is only one God purges the mind of this nonsense because the believer knows intrinsically that his life, his wealth and everything else belongs to God. All of it is on loan and will 'go back' to God eventually.

There is no more second guessing because the believer knows that no weapon, human or animal can take away his life unless God, alone has already decreed it. He knows his time of death is already fixed and that all the forces of the world combined can't take away his life even a minute before his time is due. That is why there is no braver person than the one who has pure, undivided and untainted faith in the one true God.

Nothing can scare him or her for he or she understands that everything is in God's power. Even the stress and pain of adversity, the stress of opposition, and the most fearsome military forces can't make him or her blink. When he comes out to fight for God, he is capable of taking on an enemy many times greater than himself.

How can other belief systems produce this kind of determination on such a consistent basis? Those who believe in deficient ideologies, or who believe that this world is all there is, will be more likely to think of self-preservation when faced with a desperate fight.

*Result #7*

But the most important effect of the belief that God is one and indivisible is that it makes a person obey and observe God's revealed Law without hesitation. A person who believes in God will certainly know that God is aware of everything both public and private. He will understand in a very profound way that God is the closest thing to him. If he commits a sin in the darkness of night, God knows about it. God even knows what we are thinking and even what we are intending. We can hide from everyone, but we can't hide from God. We can elude everyone, but we can't escape God's grip.

The stronger a person believes in this, the more he will actively try to observe the principles of the Godly way of life. He will avoid what his Master has forbidden and will carry out his commands, even when he is all alone with no one else to see him. This is the case because he knows that God's watchers never leave his side, and he knows and fears the day when he will be called into God's court because it will be the most comprehensive trial of his life.

This is why the first and foremost requirement of being a Muslim is to believe in no god other than the one true God. To be a Muslim means to be at peace with God. Being at peace with God, and being obedient to Him, is impossible unless we accept His overlordship and no one else's. According to the teachings of Muhammad, peace be upon him, having an accurate and firm belief in God is the most important article of faith. It is the foundation of Islam and the source of its power. All the other doctrines and regulations of Islam are centered around this core concept. Take it away and there is nothing left of Islam.

## Calling on Angels

Prophet Muhammad, peace be upon him, further instructed us to have faith in the existence of angels. This is the second article of Islamic doctrine and it is also very crucial because it cleanses the concept of monotheism from all impurities and frees it from the danger of every conceivable shade of polytheism, otherwise known as idolatry.

Throughout history, polytheists have associated two types of creatures with God:

1. *Creatures or objects that have material form and can be seen by the human eye, such as the sun, the moon, the stars, fire, mountains, animals, and even humans such as great leaders or heroes.*

2. *Creatures or objects that don't have a physical existence and are not perceptible to the human eye: the unseen beings who are believed to be engaged in the administration of the universe. For instance, there may be a god who controls the air, another who imparts light, another who brings rain, and so on.*

The alleged deities of the first type have a reference in the material world and are before humanity's gaze. The falsity of the claim that created things can be divine has already been fully exposed in our previous discussion about the meaning of the *Kalimah* — *La elaha ill Allah*. This is enough proof to dismiss the idea that material objects can enjoy a share in divinity, or deserve any reverence at all.

Now, the second type of deity, who are immaterial, are hidden from the human eye and are, therefore, full of mystery and symbolism. For this reason, polytheists are more inclined to pin their faith on them. They consider them to be supernatural manifestations, demigods and even children of a higher, supreme God. They make elaborate images, paintings and statues and render offerings to them. In order to improve our knowledge about the oneness of God, and to clear the concept of God from being tainted or mixed up with a host of lesser, unseen creatures, Islam gives us a full account of what those powers and supernatural forces (that do exist) really are.

Muhammad revealed to us that there is a class of unseen spiritual beings, whom people have misidentified as deities or gods or God's children, that are called angels. They have no share in God's divinity; they cannot deviate from His commands, even by the slightest fraction of an inch. God merely employs them to administer His Kingdom, and they carry out His orders exactly and accurately. They have no authority to do anything of their own accord; they cannot present to God any scheme conceived by themselves, they are not even authorized to intercede with God for any man. God, in fact, doesn't need them at all, but they are there, nonetheless.

144

To worship them and to solicit their help is degrading and debasing for a human being. For, on the very first day of humanity's creation, God made them bow themselves before Adam, granted to him greater knowledge than they possessed, and bestowed upon Adam the stewardship of this earth in preference to them. What debasement can, therefore, be greater for a human being than bowing himself before those who had bowed themselves before him!

Muhammad forbade us to worship angels, or to associate them with God in His divinity. He also taught us that they were loyal creatures of God, free from sin, and by their very nature unable to disobey God; they are, rather, always engaged in carrying out His orders. Moreover, he taught us that these angels of God surround us from all sides, are near to us, and are always in our company. They observe and note all our actions, good or bad. They preserve a complete record of every person's life. After death, when we will all be brought before God, they will present a full report of our life's work on earth, wherein we will find everything correctly recorded. Not a single action will be left out, however insignificant or carefully concealed it may be.

We don't know everything about the inner workings of the angels. Only some of their virtues or attributes have been mentioned to us, and we have been asked to believe in their existence. We have no other means of knowing their nature, their attributes and their qualities except through what God's prophet taught. It would therefore, be sheer folly on our part to attribute any form or quality to them of our own accord. We must believe in them exactly as we have been asked to do. To deny their existence is *kufr*. That's because we don't have any reason to deny their existence, and, secondly, our denial of them would be tantamount to attributing falsehood to Muhammad, whose validity has already been established. We believe in their existence because God's true Messenger has informed us of it.

## *A Question about Angels*

**Why did the angels have to bow down to Adam and Eve?** When God announced that He was going to make free-willed humans on earth, the angels objected saying that humans would cause trouble and be of questionable value. After God introduced Adam and Eve to the world, he gave them conscious awareness of their environment and the ability to understand the natural world. (The root word for human beings used in the Qur'an, Onns, literally means 'adaptable creature'.)

Then God called the angels to the earth and asked them to explain nature. They confessed that they didn't know anything about it. Then God told Adam to explain the names, qualities and uses of the natural world. He did a superb job. Because the angels had doubted God before, He wanted to show them they were mistaken in their estimation of humanity's worth. Then He ordered them to bow down in respect to the first human beings.

## Divine Scripture

The third article of faith which Muhammad, peace be upon him, asked us to believe in is the many scriptures or Books of God; Books which He sent down to humanity through His Prophets. God revealed His messages to prophets before Muhammad, and these books were sent down in the same way as He sent down the Qur'an to Muhammad. We have been told the names of some of these scriptures:

- **The Scrolls of Abraham**
- **The Torah of Moses**
- **The Psalms of David**
- **The Gospel of Jesus, the Messiah**

We haven't been told about any other books that might have been given to other prophets, therefore, with regard to other existing religious books that one may find around the world, we are not in a position to say with certainty whether or not they were divinely revealed scriptures. But we clearly believe that whatever Books were sent down by God were all true.

Now what of the Books whose names we have been told about? Do we believe they are still pure and intact to this day? Sadly, no. The Scrolls of Abraham no longer exist and not traceable in existing world literature. David's Psalms, the Hebrew Torah and the Aramaic Gospel are claimed by Jews and Christians to exist, but the Qur'an tells us that people have changed, added to, and even lost portions of these previous revelations. In effect, God's words have been edited, mixed up and joined with texts of people's own making.

This corruption and pollution of the former scriptures has been on such a large scale and is so evident that even Jewish and Christian scholars themselves admit that they do not possess their original texts, and have only fragments and competing versions of later day works, which have been altered over many centuries, and they are still being edited to this day! A simple comparison of a Catholic Bible, two Protestant Bibles (RSV vs. KJV) and an Orthodox Bible will prove this point quite succinctly.

Upon studying the remnants of these former scriptures, we also find that there are many passages and stories which clearly couldn't come from God. Of the rest, God's words and those of human authors are so mixed together in these books that we have no way of really knowing which sections are from God and which are from human authors.

We have been commanded to believe in previously revealed Books only in the sense of admitting that, before the Qur'an, God did also send down books through His other Prophets, and that all of them were from the same God- the same God Who also sent the Qur'an! Therefore, we can understand that the sending of the Qur'an as a Divine Book is not a new and strange event, but only confirms, restates and completes those divine instructions which people had mutilated or lost in antiquity.

The Qur'an is the last of the Divine Books sent down by God and there are some very relevant differences between it and the previous scriptures. These differences may briefly be stated as follows:

- The original texts of the former scriptures were lost altogether, and only translations of variant texts dated many centuries after the fact exist today. The Qur'an, on the other hand, exists exactly as it was revealed to the Prophet; not a word — no, not even a syllable of it — has been changed. The proof is there for all to see. There are two copies of the Qur'an still in existence that were written down within twenty years of the Prophet's passing and approved by his many surviving companions. Thus it is available in its original text. Therefore we can say with complete certainty that this final word of God has been preserved for all time.

- In the former revealed scriptures, people have mixed their own words with God's, but in the Qur'an we find only the words of God — and in their pristine purity. Even those who harbor ill-will against Islam admit that the entire book came from one source, with no evidence of mixing, interpolation or editing by other hands. In contrast, Jewish, Buddhist, Hindu and Christian scholars spend their lives studying who the many known and unknown authors and editors of their books were.

- It's historically uncertain if any of the prophets, whose names are attached to religious scriptures today, ever even had any contact with the books attributed to them. In the case of some of them it's not even known in what time frame and to which specific prophet they were revealed.

149

As for the Qur'an, the evidence that it was revealed to Muhammad is so voluminous, so convincing, so strong and so compelling that even the fiercest critics of Islam cannot cast doubt upon it. This evidence is so detailed that even the circumstances and locations where almost all of the verses and injunctions of the Qur'an were revealed are known and recorded.

• Nearly all of the former scriptures were sent down in languages which have either died out long ago, or are spoken by only a handful of people today. No nation or large community now speaks most of those languages, and of the few that have survived, there are only isolated scholars who can claim to understand them. Thus, even if those ancient holy books existed today in their original and unedited form, it would be virtually impossible in our age to correctly understand and interpret their injunctions, let alone putting them into practice in the way that they were intended. The language of the Qur'an, on the other hand, is a living language; tens of millions of people speak it, and millions more know and understand it. It is being taught and learnt in nearly every university of the world; anyone can learn it, and a person who has no time to master it can find men and women everywhere who know this language and can explain to him or her the literal meaning of the Qur'an.

• Each of the existing sacred scriptures found among the different peoples of the world has been addressed to a particular ethnic group. Each one contains a number of commands which seem to have been meant for a particular period of history and which met the needs of that society and time period only. These injunctions are neither needed today, nor can they now be smoothly and properly put into practice. A casual glance at the many

150

obscure and odd seeming laws found in the Old Testament of the Bible bears this fact out. It is evident from this and other examples that the ancient scriptures were meant specifically only for a target culture and were not meant for the world at large.

- Furthermore, they were not sent to be followed permanently by even the people they were intended for; they were meant to be acted upon only for a certain period. In contrast to this, the Qur'an is addressed to all humanity; not a single injunction within its pages can be considered as having been addressed to a particular people. In the same manner, all the commands and injunctions in the Qur'an can be acted upon at any place and in any age. This proves that the Qur'an is meant for the whole world, and is an eternal code for human life.

There's no denying the fact that all previous scriptures have defined the characteristics of what constitutes both virtue and morality; they also taught the principles of integrity and honesty and presented the method of living which leads to God's pleasure. But none of them was comprehensive enough to embrace all that is necessary for a virtuous human life.

Some of them excelled in one respect; others excelled in something else. It is the Qur'an and the Qur'an alone which enshrined not only all that was good in the former books, but also perfected the lifestyle of godliness and presented it in its entirety. It outlined the parameters of good clean living which encompasses all that is necessary for humanity on this earth.

On account of the many additions that people have made to their scriptures through the ages, many historical accounts and outright forgeries have been inserted which are against reality, revolting to reason and an affront to every instinct of justice. There are things which are cruel and unjust, and that are contradictions to morality that only serve to pollute the very purity of a person's beliefs and actions.

Furthermore, things have unfortunately been inserted that are obscene, indecent and highly immoral. The Qur'an is free of all such rubbish. It contains nothing against reason, and nothing that can be proved wrong. None of its injunctions are unjust; nothing in it is misleading.

This is the "Mountain of Light" just outside of Mecca. There is a small cave partway up the slope in which Muhammad used to retreat for meditation. It was there that he received his first revelation.

Not a trace of indecency and immorality can be found. From the beginning to the end the Book is full of wisdom and truth. It contains the best of philosophy and the choicest of law for human civilization. It points out the right path and guides people to success and salvation.

It is because of these special features of the Qur'an that all the peoples of the world have been directed to have faith in it, to give up all other previous books and to follow the Qur'an alone. The study of the differences between the Qur'an and the other previous scriptures allows us to easily see that the way of life taught in the Qur'an is not at all similar to the contradictory and mixed up theology and contents of the other books.

Faith in the truly revealed, original Books of God should be limited to the confirmation that they were all from God, were true and were sent down to fulfill, in their time, a similar purpose for which the Qur'an has been sent. On the other hand, belief in the Qur'an should be such that we accept it is purely and absolutely God's own words, that it is perfectly true, that every word of it is preserved, that everything mentioned within it is right, that it is the duty of every human being to carry out in his life each and every command of it and that whatever be against it must be rejected.

## Accepting All of God's Prophets

In the last chapter we learned that God's Messengers have been raised among every culture in ancient times, and that they all brought essentially the same message, known collectively as Islam- the religion that Prophet Muhammad, peace be upon him, also taught. In this respect all the Messengers of God belong to an identical chain and stand on par with each other. If a person confirms and believes in one of them, he or she must and ought to confirm all of them.

The reason is quite simple. Suppose ten men witnessed an event and later reported it in almost exactly the same way, with very few differences between them; if you accept the account of one of them as accurate, you automatically have to admit that what the remaining nine of them said was true. If you called any one of them a liar, by implication you would be calling all of them liars. It is for this reason that in Islam it is required to have implicit faith in all true prophets of God. Anyone who rejects even one of the true prophets would be labeled as a Kafir, though he might profess faith in some of the other prophets.

We're told in the traditions related to us from the Prophet Muhammad, peace be upon him, that the total number of all the prophets sent to the different peoples of the world at different times was 124,000. If you consider the history of the world since it was first inhabited by modern humans and the number of different cultures and nations that have passed through it, then this figure will not appear too far-fetched. We especially have to believe in those twenty five prophets whose names have been mentioned specifically in the Qur'an. Regarding the rest of those thousands of prophets, whose names and stories are virtually unknown to us, we are instructed to believe in them as well, for all prophets sent by God for the guidance of humanity were true.

Thus we believe in all the prophets raised in India, the Far East, the Middle East, Africa, Europe, the Americas and in the other regions of the world up until the time of Muhammad, peace be upon him. So what happens if we come upon an old religion, replete with a founder, beliefs and rituals, in some far off? Do we automatically accept that it is an expression of Islam (submission to God)? Not really, for we can't always judge accurately if a local religious founder was a true prophet or not. We can only do that if he was mentioned by name in the Qur'an, otherwise we have no definite way of knowing for sure.

With that said, we are not allowed to say anything against the founders of other religions. It is quite possible that some of them might have been God's Prophets, and their followers had merely corrupted their teachings after their passing, just as the followers of Moses and Jesus, peace be upon them, have done. Therefore, whenever we express any opinion about them, it can only be about the doctrines and rituals of their religions; as for the founders of those religions, we

155

will remain scrupulously silent, lest we should become guilty of irreverence towards a prophet.

There is no difference in validity among all of the true prophets for they have all been chosen by God to teach submission to His will. For this reason we, as Muslims, have been told that we must accept the truth of them all. But in spite of their equality in this respect, there are the following three differences between Muhammad and all other prophets, peace be upon them all:

- The prophets of the past were sent to certain people at certain periods of time, while Muhammad, peace be upon him, was sent for the whole world and for all times to come.

- The authentic and complete teachings of all former prophets have either disappeared altogether from the world, or whatever of them remains is not pure, and is found intermingled with many erroneous and fictitious statements. For this reason, even if someone wanted to follow their teachings in their totality, they couldn't do it. The record is corrupted and the line of transmission has been sullied. In contrast to this, the teachings of Muhammad, peace be upon him, his biography, his speeches, his lifestyle, his morals, habits, and virtues- in short, all the details of his life and work, are preserved. Muhammad, peace be upon him, therefore, is the only one of the whole line of prophets who is still something of a 'living' personality. It is still possible to follow in his footsteps correctly and confidently.

- The guidance imparted through the prophets of the past wasn't complete and all-encompassing. Former prophets were often followed by other prophets who made alterations and additions in the teachings and injunctions of their predecessors and, in this way, the chain of reforms and progress continued. That is why the teachings of the earlier prophets, after the passage of a certain amount of time, were lost in oblivion. Obviously there was no need to preserve the former teachings when amended and improved guidance had taken their place. But at long last the most perfect code of guidance was imparted to humanity through Muhammad, peace be upon him, and all previous codes were automatically abrogated, for it is futile and imprudent to follow an incomplete code when the complete code exists.

- Whoever follows Muhammad, peace be upon him, follows the best in all the prophets, for whatever was good and eternally workable in their teachings has been embodied in his teachings. Whoever, therefore, rejects and refuses to follow Muhammad's teachings and chooses to follow the lost, incomplete or corrupted message of some earlier prophet, only deprives himself of that vast amount of useful and valuable instruction and guidance that can only be found in Muhammad's teachings, teachings that never existed in the books of the earlier prophets and which was revealed only through the last of the prophets.

That's why it's now essential that each and every human being has faith in Muhammad, peace be upon him, and follow his faith alone. To become a true Muslim (to surrender to God's Will) it is necessary to have complete faith in Muhammad, peace be upon him, and to affirm that:

157

- He is a true Prophet of God.
- His teachings are absolutely perfect, free from any defect or error.
- He is the last Prophet of God. After him no other prophet will appear among any nation until the Day of Judgment, nor will any kind of equivalent person appear that Muslims will have to accept in this way.

## After Death, Life Renewed

The fifth article of the Islamic code of faith is believing in life after death. Prophet Muhammad, peace be upon him, directed us to believe in a physical resurrection after death and in a Day of Judgment. The essential ingredient of this belief is that on one set day each of our lives will end, along with everything we achieved, accomplished and worked for.

Further still, at the end of time all existence, (and every living and non-living thing,) will cease to be. Everything in the physical world will be destroyed. That day is called *Yawm ul Qiyamah*, i.e. the Last Day. On that day all the human beings who have ever lived in the world since its inception will then be restored to life and will be presented before God. He will be holding court on that day and we will be the defendants awaiting trial. The entire record of every man and woman- along with all their actions, both good and bad- will be presented before God for final judgment.

God will finally judge the record of every person to determine what fate they deserve in the next life. He will examine our faith (of lack of it) and then weigh our good and bad deeds. The one who excels in goodness will be rewarded well; the one whose sin and immorality outweigh his good deeds, (and who had little or no faith) will be punished. The reward and punishment will be administered fairly.

Those who emerge successfully from this judgment will go to paradise and the doors of eternal bliss will be opened upon them; those who are condemned and deserve punishment will be sent to Hell- the abode of fire and torture. Some will get out and enter paradise after a set term of punishment (designed to purify their souls of corruption) is endured, while some others- the worst of the worst- may find themselves remaining in torment forever.

## Why is an Afterlife Important?

Belief in life after death has always been a key part of the teachings of the prophets. Every prophet asked his followers to believe in it, in the same way the last of the prophets, Muhammad, peace be upon him, asked us to do. This has always been an essential ingredient of being a Muslim. In the same spirit, all the prophets have categorically declared that the one who disbelieves in it, or casts doubt upon it, is a concealer, or *kafir*. It is such a serious matter because denial of life after death makes all other beliefs meaningless. This denial also destroys the very motivation for leading a good life and people are driven to instead lead lives of ignorance and immorality.

Think about it: if a person really believed that this life was all there was, and nothing more, then what would hold them back from following every base whim and desire? Rather they should rape, kill, steal and do everything that suits their fancy without constraint, for there is no punishment other than facing the retribution of other humans, and what would that matter? Death would be inevitable anyway and at least the person will go with the satisfaction that he did what he wanted. No- a belief in an afterlife is what holds- what has always held- a society together, made up of upright and self-controlled individuals.

Consider the issue in another way: in your everyday life, whenever you are asked to do something, you immediately think: what do I gain by doing it and what's it going to cost me? This is the very nature of our species. We instinctively regard a useless action as totally unnecessary. We would never want to waste our time and energy in useless, wasteful, and unproductive tasks. Similarly, we don't mind doing things that are harmless to us.

And the general rule is that the deeper our conviction about the worth of a thing, the firmer will be our response to it; and the more doubtful we are about its purpose, the more wavering and shaky would be our attitude. After all, why does a child put his hand in a fire? Because he is not sure what fire will do to him. Why does he avoid studying? Because he doesn't always fully grasp the importance and benefits of education and doesn't always believe in what his elders keep trying to impress upon his mind.

Now think of the person who doesn't believe in the Day of Judgment. Wouldn't he think that it's useless to believe in God and follow a moral code of life? How much value would he assign to a life spent in the pursuit of God's pleasure? To him neither obedience to God is of any advantage, nor disobedience to Him of any harm. How would it be possible for him to ever sincerely follow the laws of God, His Prophet, and His scriptures? What incentive would there be for him to undergo all the trials and sacrifices that he would need to make just to avoid wanton worldly pleasures? If a person doesn't follow the code of God and lives according to his own likes and dislikes, then what use would there be for his belief in the existence of God, if he even had any faith at that point?

That's not all. If you will reflect still deeper, you would come to the conclusion that belief in a life after death is the greatest deciding factor in the life of a human being. Its acceptance or rejection determines the very course of his or her life and behavior. A person who thinks only of the success or failure of this world will be concerned with the benefits and drawbacks that come to him in this life only. He will not be prepared to undertake any good act if he has no hope of making a profit of some sort, nor will he be eager to avoid any wrong act if that is not particularly harmful to his interests in this world.

But a person who believes in the next world, and has a firm conviction in the final consequences of his acts, will look upon all the world - with its profits and losses - as temporary and transitory, and he won't put his eternal happiness on the line for a temporary gain. He'll look upon things in their wider perspective and will always keep the everlasting benefit or harm in view. He'll do the good, however costly it may be to him in terms of worldly gains, or however injurious it may be to his immediate interests; and he'll certainly avoid immorality, however charming it may look. He will consistently judge all things from the standpoint of their eternal consequences, and won't submit to his base whims and desires.

Thus there is a radical difference between the beliefs, approaches, and lives of the two persons. One's idea of a worthwhile action is limited to its benefits in this brief, temporary life, or as some sort of profit in the shape of money, property, public applause or other similar things which give him position, power, reputation, and worldly success. Such things become his objectives in life. Fulfillment of his own wishes and self-aggrandizement become the be-all and end-all of his life. And he doesn't prevent himself from engaging in cruelty and injustice in the pursuit of his goals. Similarly, his definition of an unfortunate move is nothing more than whatever may involve the risk of injury to his interests in this world, like loss in property or threats to his life, losing good health, losing his reputation, or some other unpleasant consequence.

> **"Whoever loves this earthly life puts a dent in their next life, and whoever loves the next life puts a dent in their earthly life, so you should prefer what is lasting to what is fleeting."**
>
> -Prophet Muhammad, peace be upon him

In contrast to this kind of person, the believer's concept of good and evil will be quite different. To him anything that pleases God is good and anything that provokes His disappointment and anger is bad. A good act, according to him, will remain good, even if it brings no benefit to him in this world, or even if it involves the loss of some worldly possession or injury to his personal interests. He'll be confident that God will reward him in the next life and that's where, he will realize, the real success lies.

Similarly, he'll not fall a prey to evil deeds merely for some worldly gain, for he knows that even if he escapes punishment in his short worldly life, he'll eventually be the loser and he won't be able to escape punishment in the court of God. He doesn't believe in the relativity of morals, but sticks to the absolute standards as revealed by God, and lives according to them irrespective of gain or injury in this word.

Thus it's the belief or disbelief in a life after death that makes people adopt different paths in life. For the one who doesn't believe in the Day of Judgment, it is absolutely impossible to fashion his life as suggested by Islam. Islam says: "Give charity to the poor for the sake of God." His answer will be: "No, charity will decrease my fortune; instead, I'll make some more investments and live off the interest!" And while he sits back and collects his fees, he will give little thought to how much the poor and hungry debtors are suffering.

Islam says: "Always speak the truth and avoid lying, even though you might gain by deceit, or lose by speaking the truth." But his reply would be: "Well, what can I do? Telling the truth is of no use to me here. If I can avoid harm or gain some benefit, then why shouldn't I lie?" When a person passes by on a deserted street and finds money or valuables lying there, in such a situation Islam says: "This is not your property, don't take it for yourself."

But a worldly-oriented person would say: "All right! Look what I found! Out of the blue! Why shouldn't I take it? No one is around to see me pick it up. No one will report me to the police or give evidence against me in a court of law. Why shouldn't I make use of this lucky find?"

If someone secretly gave some money to his friend, but then died before he could collect it back, then what should be done? Islam would say: "Be honest with the money that was given for you to hold. Turn it over to the heirs of the deceased." A worldly-oriented person would say quite the contrary: "Why give it back? There's no proof that he kept his money with me; his family doesn't know about it. If I can keep the money without any trouble, without any fear of legal claim, or stain upon my reputation, why shouldn't I do it?"

How different the responses are to so many moral questions and it all depends on whether or not you focus on this life exclusively, or you think about consequences that will befall you even after this life is through.

During every stage of one's life, Islam directs us to follow the path of morality; and as time goes by, and as our faith in the rightness of our lifestyle increases, we will come to the point where we will never willingly want to swerve towards any hint of immorality. Islam measures and considers

A Muslim is taught that life is a brief gift from the Creator. We live for a time and are given the chance to perfect our souls making us worthy of heaven. Our conscience is a sign of God's existence

165

everything from the viewpoint of its everlasting consequence, while a worldly-oriented person only has in view the immediate and earthly outcome of any action or plan.

Now, you can understand why a person can't really be a Muslim without believing in the Day of Judgment. To be a Muslim is an organic thing because it requires life affirmation, spiritual growth and moral development. The fact is that no one can become a truly righteous person without this belief, for the denial of the Day of Judgment drains the life-blood of humanity from our hearts and brings us down to a place even lower than that of the most savage beasts and animals.

## The Proof for the Afterlife

So far we've discussed the need and importance of a belief in the Day of Judgment. Now let's consider the rational proofs for this belief. As you will see, what Muhammad, peace be upon him, taught us about life after death is clearly rational and logical. Although our belief in an afterlife and a Day of Judgment is based upon our implicit faith in the Messenger of God, rational reflection not only confirms this belief but also reveals that Muhammad's teachings in this respect are much more reasonable and understandable than all other viewpoints in this area. In our world today, there are many competing teachings about what happens after death. They can be enumerated as follows:

1.  Some people say that there's nothing left of a human being after death, and that after this life-ending event, there's no other realm of existence. According to them, belief in anything beyond death has no basis in reality. They say that there's no possibility of it and such a belief is quite unscientific. "Science" is often called upon to provide proof.

2.  Another group of people maintains that human beings, in order to bear the consequences of their life's actions, are repeatedly reincarnated back into this world. If he or she leads a bad life, in the next incarnation of life they might assume the shape of an animal, like a dog, bug, or cat, or they might become a tree or something else lower than a human. If his or her life was moral and good, then he or she will be reborn as a human again, but into a higher caste, or social level. After thousands of years of recycling through life, they might achieve a kind of nothingness and be released into the cosmos. This viewpoint is found in most Eastern religions.

3.  The last viewpoint involves a belief in a Day of Judgment, a resurrection, a review of one's faith and works in a Divine Court and then the administration of reward and punishment. This doctrine was taught by all Prophets and is common in Western religions.

Now let's consider each of these viewpoints in turn. The first position, which took to itself the authority and support of science, alleges that there is no reality in a life after death. Its supporters say that they have never seen anybody who has come back from the dead and told us about another realm of existence. Their reasoning goes something like this: "We see that after death a human being is reduced to dust. Therefore death is the end of life and there is no life after death."

167

But just think about this kind of logic! Is this really a scientific style of deduction? Is this kind of claim really built upon sound reasoning? If they've never heard of any case of a dead person returning from the grave to give us a report, then all they can say is that they don't know what will happen after death. But, instead of remaining within this limit, they declare that nothing will happen after death, at the same time they allege that they speak out of tested fact! But the real fact is that they are merely making pronouncements based on ignorance.

Science tells us nothing negative or positive in this respect and their assertion that life after death has no truth to it is totally unfounded. Their reasoning is not any different to an ignoramus who has never seen an atom and who, based on that "knowledge," suddenly proclaims that atoms have no existence at all! If a person hasn't seen something with their own eyes, it doesn't necessarily mean that it doesn't exist. No one can claim that something is real or not just because they haven't seen it personally. This claim is illusionary and is thoroughly unscientific. No reasonable person can give it any weight.

Now look to beliefs of the second group. According to them, a person just happens to be a human being simply because in his previous animal form he had done some good deeds. On the flip side, an animal is an animal simply because previously (as a human being) he had behaved badly. In other words, to be a human or an animal is the consequence of one's deeds in their previous form.

Well, one may ask, "Which of them existed first, the human or animal?" If they say humans came before animals, and merely began regressing downwards, then they will have to backtrack and agree that there must have been animals even before that, who did good deeds in order to make humans. If they say it was the animals who came first, then they will have to concede that there must have been a human before that who transformed into an animal on account of his bad deeds. This puts us into a vicious of: 'What came first, the chicken or the egg?' If the advocates of this belief can't settle on which form came first, because every generation that exists implies a preceding generation so that the succeeding generation may be considered as the consequence of the former... This is all simply absurd.

Now consider the last viewpoint. Its first proposition is this: "This world will one day come to an end. God will put the brakes on nature and erase the universe, and in its place will evolve another more highly developed and far superior cosmos."

We hold that scientifically, the underlying foundation of this statement is undeniably true. No doubt can be cast upon its veracity. What is our proof? Consider this: the more we reflect upon the nature of the cosmos, the more clearly it is proved that the existing galactic system is not permanent and everlasting. Indeed, all the forces of nature working throughout the universe are limited in their scope, and it is a certainty that one day all the energy released by the Big Bang will be completely exhausted. Through evidence they have collected and tested, scientists agree that one day the sun will become cold and will lose all its energy; the galaxies, which are all moving away from each other, will begin to contract back together one day and will eventually collide with one another. Many years hence the whole system of the universe will be upset and destroyed.

As a side point, there are those who claim that all life just evolved on earth by a lucky accident. Their basic operating principle is that through natural selection forms constantly improve into better and more dynamic things. Well, if evolution is considered a scientific truth on one planet in this universe, then why shouldn't it be true for the whole of it? Why should the universe collapse in upon itself and become non-existent when it also can "evolve" and grow into some other, superior form? So, using science as our guide, we have proven that the prophetic teachings are based upon facts: the universe, as we know it, will be destroyed, but its mass and matter will not just disappear, it will transform into a new form- the size and shape of which we cannot even begin to understand.

The second claim of this belief in an afterlife is that: "Every human being will be given life again after their physical death." Is it impossible? If it is, then how is human life possible at all in the first place? Some claim we are merely a happy accident that evolved haphazardly over two billion years without any Divine direction or tinkering. Statistics have shown that it is more likely for all the scattered pieces of a car to assemble themselves than for all the right conditions to be met to produce a human being in all its glory. Given this reality, it is not any more far-fetched to say that a living God created human beings in this world, and that One with that kind of power can easily do so again in another realm of existence. Not only is that a possibility, it is also a positive necessity, as will be show later.

The next principle we come upon is that: "The record of all the actions of each and every one of us in this world is preserved and will be presented on the Day of Resurrection." Is it possible for the "memory" of every action to be preserved? The proof of the validity of this proposition is provided here, today, by science itself. In more ancient days, people thought that whatever sounds we made simply traveled through the air for a time and then died out. Now, it has been discovered that sounds leave slight impressions upon surrounding objects and that, with the right kind of equipment, they can be reproduced. Our technology allows us to even "capture" real life sounds and record them on compact disks and other media.

In addition, movements of objects leave impressions in the very air itself. The body heat from a person passing through a room makes a permanent change in its composition that can be measured long after. As for light, it travels forever at a constant rate. From just these few examples it can be clearly seen that the record of every human being's movements, words and actions is being impressed upon all things which come into contact with the unseen waves produced by their activities. This shows that the record of our entire life's deeds is completely preserved and can be reproduced-by the right source.

The next part of the prophetic position is as follows: "On the Day of Resurrection God will assemble His court of justice, and with complete fairness He will reward or punish people based upon their faith and the quality of their life's works." What is so unreasonable about that? Reason itself demands that, if there was a God, then He ought to examine us and pronounce His fair judgment, otherwise, why was the principle of justice so ingrained in our very social and psychological make up. Why do we, of all creatures, ruminate on equity, fairness, compensation, reward, retribution and all the other principles associated with justice? If there is a standard of justice then that means there is an ultimate arbiter of justice.

Look at it this way, when we look around us in our world every day, we see that there are many people who do selfless, noble acts of kindness and generosity, and yet they receive no compensation for it. We also see that there are many people who do horrible, terrible crimes, but they often don't seem to suffer any penalty for it here. Not only this, we see that there are many cases, every day, of good people, honest people, who help out, who sacrifice and share, and then get nothing but heartache and stress on account of it. On the flip side, we see many bad people, crooks and abusers, who get away with their misdeeds and even gain success on account of them. Where is the justice in that? When we notice these injustices happening every day, our reason and sense of fairness demand that a time must come when the person who does good must be rewarded and the one who does evil and hurts others must be punished.

The way this world works, as you can see for yourself, is through the interplay of material forces. A person who wants to do evil, and who has the means to do it, can carry out his plan and affect everyone and everything around him. He may even get away with his evil deeds if there is nothing in the material world that says he must be punished or stopped (other than the laws people have enacted which are based, quite curiously enough, on ancient prophetic religious laws, but even then many criminals beat the system or benefit when the system is broken). If you have a can of gas and a match, you can set fire to your enemy's house and can escape every consequence of this deed, if "luck" is in your favor. Does that mean that such a crime has no consequences at all? Certainly not! It means only that its physical manifestation has appeared and that its penalty will be reserved for later.

Do you really think that it's a reasonable proposition that justice could never be served? If you say it should be served then the question is where? Certainly not in this world because in the physical world only the physical consequences of actions manifest themselves fully, while moral results are often muddled. The fullest result of this higher level of retribution can appear only if there comes into existence another order of things wherein rational and moral laws reign supreme and occupy the governing position and where all physical laws are made subject to them. That is the next world which, as we have said before, is the next evolutionary stage of the universe.

It's evolutionary, in this sense, that it will be governed by moral laws rather than by physical laws. The rational consequences of humanity's actions, which are reserved wholly or partly in this world, will appear therein. Our status will be determined by our rational and moral worth as judged in accordance with our conduct in this life of testing and trials. There you will not find a qualified person serving under a fool, or a moral person chafing under the thumb of a pervert, as is the case in this world.

The last claim of this prophetic doctrine is the existence of Paradise and Hell, which is also not impossible. If God can make the sun, the moon, the stars and the earth, why wouldn't He be able to make a Paradise and a Hell? When He holds His court and pronounces His judgment, rewarding the meritorious and punishing the guilty, there must be a place where the righteous might enjoy their reward in honor, happiness and gratification, and another place wherein the condemned might feel their due share of humility, pain and misery.

After considering all these questions no reasonable person can escape the conclusion that the belief in a life after death is the most acceptable to reason and common sense, and that there is nothing in it which can be said to be unreasonable or impossible. Moreover, when a qualified and proven prophet like Muhammad, peace be upon him, has stated this to be a fact, (and it involves nothing but what is good for us,) wisdom lies in believing it implicitly and not in rejecting it without any sound reason.

# The Seven Core Beliefs of Islam

**Monotheism**. God is one with no partners, children or spouses. He was never born on earth, nor has He ever died. The phrase, "La elaha ill Allah," meaning, "There is no god but the God," is the defining statement of Islam's uncompromising purity of monotheism.

**The Angels**. They are assigned functions in the universe. They are not male or female, but can assume various forms and guises. They do not have free will. They are made of light energy. They never disobey God.

**The Books (Revealed Scriptures) of God**. God has revealed organized bodies of scripture to prophets at various times in the past. The Torah, the Psalms and the Gospel of Jesus are all considered to be true revelations. The original revelations have been lost or edited beyond all recognition, however. The Qur'an is God's last revelation and supersedes all past scriptures.

**The Prophets**. God has chosen humans to be the bearers of His messages to other humans. This is because any supernatural occurrence would bias our test of faith in this life by dampening our need to develop faith in what we cannot see yet.

**The Last Day**. This is the belief that human civilization will end one day and all of the souls of every human being who ever lived will be brought to life again.

**God's Foreknowledge**. God is outside of any timelines, for He created Time. He knows the past, present and future and knows what our futures hold.

**Life after Death**. After the Last Day, when all souls will be awakened and reunited with a new body, they will have to stand for judgment before God. Heaven or Hell will await us after that as our just recompense.

What we've discussed here in this chapter are the five articles of faith which form the foundation for the superstructure of Islam. When you declare *La elaha ill Allah* (there is no god but the God), you give up all false deities and profess that you're a creature of the One God. And when you add these words, *Muhammadar-Rasulullah*, (Muhammad is God's Messenger), you confirm and accept the Prophethood of Muhammad, peace be upon him.

With the admission of his Prophethood it becomes obligatory that you should believe in the divine nature and attributes of God, in His angels, in His revealed Books, and in life after death, and earnestly follow that method of obeying God and serving Him which Prophet Muhammad, peace be upon him, has asked us to follow. Herein lays the road to success and salvation.

# 5
# Faith in Action

As we've learned in the previous chapter, Prophet Muhammad, peace be upon him, taught that we should believe in five specific doctrines as the basis for our faith. These are:

- To believe in one God, Who has absolutely no associate with Him in His divinity.

- To believe that God created angels to serve Him.

- To believe in the many scriptures revealed by God, and in the Holy Qur'an as His last revealed Book of Divine Guidance.

- To believe in all of the many prophets of God, and to accept that Muhammad, peace be upon him, was God's last Messenger to the world.

- To believe in life after death.

These five doctrines make up the foundation of Islam. Whoever believes in them enters into the fellowship of the Muslim community. But a mere verbal profession alone doesn't make a person a complete Muslim. To become a complete Muslim one has to fully carry out in practice the instructions given by Muhammad, peace be upon him, as ordained by God, for if a person believes in God then practical obedience to Him is the next logical step; and it's obedience to God which constitutes the basis for the religion of Islam. Through an active expression of belief in your daily life and habits you acknowledge without a doubt that God alone is your sole object of devotion. This also shows that you accept Him as your Creator and that you understand completely that you are His creature: He is your Master, and you are His slave; He is your Ruler and you are His subject. After having acknowledged Him as your Master and Ruler, if you refuse to obey Him, then you're a rebel against God by your own admission.

Along with having faith in God's Lordship over your life, your conviction instills in you the realization that the Qur'an is God's Book, and that all of its contents are revealed guidance from God. Thus it becomes your duty to accept and obey whatever is contained within it. In a complimentary fashion, you have also accepted that the bearer of the Qur'an, Muhammad, peace be upon him, is God's Messenger, which also means that you've accepted that each and every one of his teachings and principles are from God. After these successive acknowledgements, obedience to Him becomes your primary duty. Therefore you can only be a full-fledged Muslim when your practice is consistent with your profession; otherwise your Islam will remain incomplete.

So let's now turn to the code of conduct that Muhammad, peace be upon him, taught, keeping in mind that whatever he brought was in accordance with the will of God Almighty. The first element of the code concerns daily acts of devotion, worship and spiritual renewal techniques that God has ordained for us to keep our hearts on the path of faith, (and also to keep our minds off of immorality and the overwhelming temptations of this life!) These are duties that are incumbent on each and every Muslim to follow.

## How Do We Serve God?

In the Arabic language there is a word known as 'Ibadah. It is derived from the word for 'servant' and literally means (in the religious sense) acts of service owed to God. It implies that God is our Master and that we are His servants. In the old sense of this type of relationship, whatever a servant did in obedience to (and for the pleasure of his Master) was a due act of service that he was obligated to perform joyfully. The Islamic concept of service to God is much broader than that. God-oriented service can be as simple as learning not to use foul language, avoiding lies, learning not to abuse people or desiring only to speak honestly and gently. Since God's rules encompass even this level of personal action, being mindful with one's manners is also a form of service to God.

If you obey the law of God in both letter and in spirit in your commercial dealings and career paths, and abide by it in your dealings with your parents, relatives, friends and all those who come into contact with you -

all of these activities as well constitute service to God. If you help the poor and the destitute, give food to the hungry, and serve the ailing and the afflicted, and do all of this, not for any personal gain of yours, but only to seek the pleasure of God, then they're nothing short of acts of Godly service as well. Even your economic activities, the activities you undertake to earn your living and to feed your dependants, are acts of service, as long as you remain honest and truthful in your conduct and observe the principles set forth by your Creator.

In short, all of your worldly activities and even the trends you promote throughout your entire life are part of your service to God, provided that your life's accomplishments and activities are in accordance with the laws of God, and that your heart is filled with fear of displeasing Him, and finally that your ultimate objective in undertaking all theses activities is to seek the pleasure of God. And so, whenever you do good or avoid evil out of the fear of God, in whatever sphere of life you engage in, you are discharging your Islamic obligations. This is the essential spirit of Service to God, and it confirms your commitment to the ideal of total submission to the pleasure of God. Through Service to God you craft your entire life according to the rhythm and flow of Islam, not leaving out even the most insignificant part of your daily existence.

To help achieve this goal of living for the pleasure of our Maker, a set of formal rites and rituals has been constituted which serves as a course in moral training, if you will. The more faithfully we follow this spiritual training program, the better equipped we will be to weather the many storms and temptations of life which seek to distract us and make us lose our way. The Acts of Service, then, are thus the pillars on which the edifice of Islam rests.

## Prayer: the Path to Inner Peace

The most important daily obligation for a Muslim to perform is what is known as *Salat*, or Prayer. *Salat* literally means 'to make a connection to something,' and in this sense, when we perform our prayers we are establishing a 'connection' to God. In the Islamic form of prayer, we repeat and refresh in our hearts, five times a day, the realization that God is our sovereign and that we owe obedience only to Him.

Imagine, if you will, that you are a Muslim. Before the break of dawn you arise to praise God. You wash your face and hands and feet to be ritually pure and then present yourself before your Lord for prayer. The various postures of standing, bowing and prostrating that you assume during your prayers are the very embodiment of the spirit of submission; the different prayers and supplications that you utter remind you of your commitments to your God. You seek His guidance and ask Him again and again to enable you to avoid His displeasure and follow His chosen path. You read out from the Book of the Lord and witness to the truth of the Prophet, and you also refresh your belief in the Day of

Judgment and enliven in your memory the fact that you have to appear before your Lord and give an account of your entire life. This is how your day starts everyday: with serenity, reminders of faith and tranquility.

Then, by noon time, when you're ready to contemplate the middle of your day, you hear the words of a Prayer-Caller over a loudspeaker, calling you to prayers once more and again you submit to your God and renew your covenant with Him. You dissociate yourself from your worldly engagements for a few moments and seek an audience with God. This once again brings to the front of your mind your real role in life. Then, after this rededication, you go back to whatever it was you were doing. A few hours later, in the late afternoon, you once again are asked to remember God. This acts as a further reminder to you and once more you can refocus your attention on the meaning and purpose of your faith.

When the sun sets and the darkness of the night begins to descend upon the world, you again submit yourself to God in prayer so that you won't forget your duties and obligations to Him in the midst of the approaching shadows of the evening. And then, after the last rays of light have disappeared from the sky you again appear before your Lord to perform your last prayer of the day. Thus before going to sleep you once again renew your faith and prostrate before your God. And this is how you complete your day. The frequency and timings of the prayers never let the object and mission of life be lost sight of in the maze of worldly activities.

On a very basic level, it's fairly easy to understand how the daily prayers can strengthen the foundations of your faith, how they can help prepare you to follow a life of virtue and obedience to God, and how they can refresh the kinds of life-affirming beliefs from which spring courage, sincerity, purposefulness, purity of heart, advancement of the soul, and enrichment of morals. Now let's look deeper into how these and other benefits are actually played out in the daily life of a Muslim.

Before you can begin any prayer, you must first do a kind of ritual washing of the head, hands and feet called Wudu, or ablution. As you perform it, in the way prescribed by the Holy Prophet, it serves to both refresh the senses and also to bring home to us the importance of presenting ourselves before our Creator cleansed and pure. Next, when you actually begin to say your prayers, you do them according to the instructions of the Prophet.

Why do you follow the prayer format that he taught? Mainly because you believe in the prophethood of Muhammad, peace be upon him, and hold it as your duty to follow him without question. You wouldn't even think of messing around with the order or recited script of the many formulas for praise and supplication that you recite throughout the prayer, and that's because you regard the Qur'an as the very Word of God and would consider it a sin to be loose or casual with it.

# What do Muslims Say in their Prayers?

*1.* **Supplications.** *There are many supplications, or requests to God for forgiveness or mercy that are said in the Islamic prayers. One example is:* "O God, I have wronged my own soul greatly, and no one can forgive sins other than You. So forgive me with Your forgiveness and have mercy upon me. Surely You are the Forgiving and the Merciful."

*2.* **Praise.** *God is praised in many forms and in many ways in Islamic prayers. Here is one phrase that is said:* "Glory to you, O God, and praise is only for You. Exalted are Your Holy Names and high is Your greatness. There is no other god than You."

*3.* **The Most Important Prayer.** *In every prayer the opening chapter of the Qur'an is recited. It is the 'Lord's Prayer' of the Muslims. It goes as follows:* "In the Name of God, the Compassionate Source of All Mercy. Praise be to God, the Lord of the Universe; the Compassionate Source of All Mercy and Master of the Day of Judgment. We serve You alone and look to You alone for help. Guide us along the straight path, the path of those whom You have favored, not the path of those who've earned Your anger, nor of those who've gone astray.
(Qur'an 1:1-7)

*4.* **Benedictions.** *In our daily prayers we bring to mind the noble qualities of God's prophets, specifically Abraham and Muhammad.*

In the prayers you recite many things quietly to yourself. If you didn't say them at all or purposely said them improperly, there would be no one to check up on you. But you, again, would never intentionally do such a disrespectful and dishonest thing. Why? Because you believe that God is ever watchful and He listens to all that you say (and you also know that He's aware of everything open and secret.)

If you were all alone and the next prayer time became due upon you, what makes you offer your prayers when there is no one to tell you to do it, or even to see you offering them? Isn't it because of your heartfelt belief that God is always watching you? What makes you leave your lucrative business affairs or important errands and rush towards the mosque for prayers?

What makes you interrupt your deepest sleep in the early hours of the morning to go to the mosque, or in the heat of the afternoon sun or to leave your evening relaxation time for the sake of prayers? Is it anything other than a sense of duty- your realization that you must fulfill your responsibility to the Lord, come what may? And why are you so concerned about making even a small mistake in your prayers? Because your heart is filled with the fear of God. You know that you have to appear before Him on the Day of Judgment and give an account of your entire life and you don't want to feel ashamed because of your own shortcomings.

Now just think about it for a moment. Can there be a better course of moral and spiritual training than prayers? It is this very kind of frequent and structured training that can transform a human being into a perfect Muslim. Prayer reminds each of us about our covenant with God, it refreshes our faith in Him, and it keeps the awareness of Judgment Day alive and ever-present before our mind's eye. It encourages us follow the Prophet's noble example and it trains us in the observance of our duties.

This is indeed a structured training program for conforming one's practice to one's ideals. Obviously, if a person's consciousness of his or her duties towards their Creator was so acute that they prize pleasing Him above all worldly gains and keep on refreshing this goal through prayers, then they would certainly be on the straight and narrow in all of their worldly dealings. Otherwise they will be inviting the displeasure of God which they've always tried their best to avoid.

The sincere believer will abide by the law of God throughout the course of their entire life in the same way that he or she learned to adhere to the punctual and serious nature of the five daily prayers. This kind of motivated and disciplined person can always be relied upon to be moral and upright in other fields of endeavor as well, for if the shadow of dishonesty or deceit approaches him, he will try to avoid them at all costs for fear of the Lord which would be an ever present factor in his heart. And even if, after such a rigorous training program like Salah is made a part of his life, a person still misbehaves in some area of his life or another, and disobeys the laws of God, it will be plain to see that the fault for this shortcoming can be none other than a lack of faith at the core of his heart, or some other similar defect in his mind or understanding.

Not all prayers are individual in nature. There is one special prayer service per week when Muslims are asked to come together in fellowship, mutual love and understanding. This is called *Salatul Jumu'ah*, or the Friday congregational prayer. This community gathering creates among Muslims a bond of loyalty and mutual awareness. It arouses in them the sense of their collective unity and fosters among them a kind of spiritual fraternity. As a group they say their prayers in one congregation and this inculcates in them a deep feeling of brotherhood and sisterhood.

Prayers are also a symbol of equality in Islam, for the rich and the poor, the low and the high, the rulers and the ruled, the educated and the illiterate, the black, the brown, the yellow and the white- everyone stands equally in anonymous rows, shoulder to shoulder with no preference by race, prostrating before their Lord. The Friday prayer also inculcates in Muslims a strong sense of discipline and obedience to the chosen leader, as one man is appointed to deliver a sermon to inspire Muslims and foster in them a sense of hope and humbleness. Following this, the congregation lines up behind this very same preacher and follows his lead in prayer. In short, prayer trains Muslims in all of those virtues which

187

make it possible to develop a richly satisfying individual as well as collective life.

These are but a few of the many benefits we can derive from regularly performing the daily prayers. If we refuse to avail ourselves of these free gifts then we're only cheating ourselves. Now if we aren't performing the prescribed daily prayers it can only mean one of two things: either we don't yet know that prayer is our duty, or we do know about the requirement, but we're choosing to ignore it.

In that case our claim to faith would be a shameless lie, for if we refuse to take orders we no longer acknowledge the Authority. In the second case, if we recognize the Authority, and still flout His Commands, then we're the most unreliable creature that ever walked upon the earth! For if we can be dishonest to the highest authority in the universe, what guarantee is there that we won't do the same in our dealings with other human beings? And if two-timing overwhelms a society, what a pit of misery and chaos it's bound to become!

## Fasting and Self-Discipline

What the prayers seek to achieve five times daily, fasting in the Islamic month of Ramadan does once a year. During this period we consume neither food nor drink from dawn to dusk, no matter how delicious the dish or how hungry or thirsty we feel. What is it that makes us voluntarily undergo such a hardship for thirty days? It's nothing less than our sincere faith in God, our fear of displeasing Him, and our contemplation of the Day of Judgment. Each and every moment during our fast we suppress our passions and desires and thereby proclaim the supremacy of the Law of God.

This great test keeps us conscious of our duty and thus strengthens our faith. By denying ourselves what our bodies crave most we build up a deep reservoir of patience and perseverance. Coming face to face- on a daily basis- with feelings of want forces us to develop self-discipline in order to weather the test. Fasting brings us face to face with the realities of life and helps us make our lives, during the rest of the year, lives oriented towards true subservience to His Will.

Taken from another point of view, fasting also has an immense impact upon the ebb and flow of society at large. All Muslims, irrespective of their wealth or class, must observe the same type of fast during the same month. This brings to prominence the essential equality of all men and women and thus goes a long way towards creating in the community fraternal feelings of sisterhood and brotherhood.

During this holy month of Ramadan, immorality diminishes while virtue seems to spring from every heart, and the whole atmosphere is filled with piety and purity. This discipline has been imposed upon us to our own advantage, and those who don't fulfill this duty have shown that they are not willing to undergo a minor hardship for the sake of self-improvement.

# More on Fasting

1. When is Ramadan? Islam has a religious calendar based on the thirty day lunar cycle. There are twelve months in an Islamic year and the ninth month is the month of Ramadan.

2. What is the procedure? From just before dawn until sunset, Muslims are required to abstain from all food, liquids, sexual relations, and even smoking (if the person is a smoker, which is generally considered to be forbidden by most Muslim scholars anyway). In addition, a Muslim is particularly asked to not argue with anyone, not to tell a lie, not to use foul language and not to get into any fights. These things are sins in Islam anyway, but the Muslim is told that God might not count their fasting if they do them, so Muslims are on their best behavior. This serves to make them conscious of these sins so they can learn to avoid them outside of Ramadan as well. After sunset until just before dawn Muslims can eat, drink and engage in intimate activities.

3. Does Anything Special Happen in Ramadan? In Ramadan, Muslims try to read one out of thirty parts of the Qur'an each day. This is in remembrance of the fact that the revelation of the Qur'an began in this month to Prophet Muhammad, peace be upon him, in the year 610 CE. Every night there is also a special service held in the mosques where people can pray while an Imam, or prayer leader, recites the Qur'an. Families usually have elaborate dinner parties after sunset and after the month is finished there is a big holiday called 'Eidul Fitr', which means the Festival of the Fast-breaking.

4. What is the Reward? The application of spiritual and practical lessons for our lives is a major step forward in understanding. We learn that all life depends upon God's bounty as evidenced by our dependence on the food and drink we need every day to survive. We learn to develop self-discipline and learn to conquer the hold our more animalistic desires and urges have upon us. We learn to feel sorry for the poor and this makes us more likely to want to help them. Our sense of morality grows as well. Contemplation and a clear picture of the shortness of this life bring richness to our lives as we learn to appreciate what we have. Beyond that, discharging this duty laid upon us from God absolves us of all of our previous sins and paves the way for entrance into heaven in the next life.

## Charity for All

The third obligation upon the life of a Muslim is a practice called *Zakat*. *Zakat* is often translated into English as charity, but the actual meaning of the word is much closer to the idea of purifying one's self. Here's how it works: every Muslim, whose financial assets are above a certain specified minimum, must donate the value of 2.5% annually of his or her net savings and assets to charity.

Deserving persons and causes include: supporting poor people and the unemployed, helping new converts who may have suffered hardships on account of their conversion, giving a hand to a stranded traveler, supporting orphans and widows or helping people get out of debt. This 2.5% is just the minimum that one has to pay, however. As Muslims we are encouraged to donate as much as we can to help those who are less fortunate than us. The more you give the greater the reward that God will bestow upon you either in this life, the next, or both!

The money that we pay as *Zakat* is not considered to be something that God needs or receives. He is above any want or desire. In His infinite mercy He promises us tremendous rewards if we help our fellows. But there is a catch: in order to receive God's reward and credit, we must give our charity in God's Name, reminding us that we should not expect, nor demand, any worldly compensation or paybacks from the people we are helping, nor should we desire to be known far and wide as generous people.

*Zakat* is as much a part of Islamic practice as any other form of spiritual discipline such as prayer or fasting. Its main importance lies in the fact that is fosters in us the qualities of sacrifice and rids us of selfishness and greed. Islam wants to create the kind of person who is ready to give in God's cause from their hard-earned money willingly and without expecting any personal or worldly gain. Islam does not approve of greedy misers. A true Muslim will, when the call comes, sacrifice his belongings in the way of God, for *Zakat* has already trained him to be ready to let loose the baggage of this life willingly and without regret.

Society at large also benefits from the institution of *Zakat*. It is the duty of every Muslim of means to help those who are less fortunate, whether they are Muslims or not. A person's wealth is not meant to be spent solely on one's own comfort and luxury, for there are rightful claimants upon his bounty. They are the widows and orphans, the poor and disabled and those who can't find work. They are those who have talent and intelligence but who have gotten a rough deal in life. The one who doesn't recognize the right that such members of his community hold over him are indeed cruel, for there is no greater cruelty than to fill one's own bank account while the masses suffer from hunger and deprivation.

Islam is the sworn enemy of this kind of selfishness and greed. Those who conceal the truth of God's love in their hearts look upon wealth as something to hold on to with no thought of sharing it. Rather they use debt and interest to hoard more and more. The teachings of Islam seek to instill a completely opposite attitude. They tell a person to share his or her wealth with others and to help them to stand up on their own so they can become productive members of just society themselves.

## The Pilgrim's Road

The fourth form of spiritual exercise a Muslim must perform is a once-in-a-lifetime pilgrimage to the holy city of Mecca, in Arabia. This duty, called the Hajj, is valid upon all those who are physically able and who can afford to undertake it. In the center of the city of Mecca is a small shrine that was originally built by Prophet Abraham to be a center of worship dedicated to the one true God. On account of his great faithfulness, God rewarded Abraham by declaring that that shrine, known as the *Ka'bah*, or Cube, would be His focal point for all humanity. Today, all Muslims perform their prayers facing the direction of Mecca.

Our visit to this place is not just for mere tourism, though. This ritual pilgrimage has its own set of practices and conditions to be fulfilled with the result being that purity and goodness are further accentuated within our being. When we undertake to perform the pilgrimage, we must suppress our passions, refrain from all forms of violence both physical and verbal, and we must work diligently to purify our words and deeds.

Nothing less than the forgiveness of all our sins is promised to us by God as a result of all of our sincerity and effort.

The holy sanctuary at Mecca during night prayers  The *Ka'bah* was built originally by Prophet Abraham and has been rebuilt many times over the last several thousand years.  Currently over two million people make the *Hajj* annually.

In a way, since it involves so many facets of spiritual training, the pilgrimage can be considered one of the greatest forms of service to God. Think about it: unless a person really loved God with all his heart, he would never consent to going on such a long journey, leaving behind his friends and family, just to walk around in the desert and beseech God's forgiveness. This pilgrimage is unlike any other journey anyone can ever make, for all throughout its arduous tasks, a person's thoughts are concentrated on God and his inner core vibrates with the thrill of intense devotion.

When the pilgrim reaches the holy sanctuary, he will find the atmosphere filled with purity and godliness. All around him he will see the places and sites which are an integral part of the history of his faith. All of this leaves a deep impression upon his mind which he will carry with him for the rest of his life.

There are many benefits that a faithful and sincere Muslim will gain from this experience. In addition to the spiritual rewards, Mecca is something like the central hub in the world of Islam. Muslim from all corners of the world get the opportunity to meet one another, to discuss topics of common interest, to refresh their faith and to reinforce the concept that all people are equal regardless of race or ethnic group. They regenerate that fundamental idea that everyone deserves the love and sympathy of their fellows regardless of where they came from or how wealthy or poor they are. Thus, the pilgrimage unites the Muslims of the world into one international brotherhood.

## The Struggle for Justice

Although it is not mentioned as a spiritual discipline in the Islamic framework of service to God, the principle that Muslims should and ought to defend themselves is an oft-repeated theme in the Qur'an and in the recorded sayings of Muhammad, peace be upon him. Besides being an obviously permissible concept in the law of nature, self-defense is also a test of our sincerity as followers of Islam. If we decline to defend a friend of ours against plots and attacks from his enemies, nor show any care for his welfare, then we would be a false friend indeed!

In the same way, if we say we believe in Islam, or submission to the Will of God, then we must eagerly guard and uphold the integrity and safety of Islamic knowledge and also of Muslim people. Our guide must be the preservation and the best interests of all those who are faithful to God and our own personal wants and needs must come second. This is being faithful to our cause and creed.

## Just What is *Jihad* Anyway?

*Jihad*. Today there is perhaps no more misunderstood word than this, both among Muslims and non-Muslims. In the first instance, the word Jihad doesn't mean war or violence of any kind. It literally means to struggle or strive to achieve a goal. Someone who exerts him or her self physically or mentally to get some kind of result, or even someone who spends his money to further their education in the cause of God is doing a kind of Jihad.

Jihad can also apply to the conduct of war in the sense that the combatants are giving their all for the cause they believe in, but Jihad doesn't mean war, and certainly not war of the aggressive, offensive kind. Jihad is a part of the overall defense of Islam and Muslims. It can be applied only in three specific circumstances. These are:

1. When the Muslim community is attacked, then they must defend themselves.
2. If an evil tyrant is oppressing their people then Muslims must come to the rescue.
3. If a foreign government restricts the free practice of religion then Muslims are obligated to remove that government or get it to change its policies so all people can have access to the teachings of God. [1]

The supreme sacrifice of actually putting one's life on the line for a noble cause is the responsibility of all Muslims, though if at least some people are organized to face an outside evil, then the rest of the community is exempt from this duty. On the flip side, if no one comes forward to defend Islam and fight oppression and tyranny, then the entire community is held in dereliction of duty. The concession that allows only a few to participate in Jihad is nullified if the Islamic community

---

[1] The Islamic rules of warfare dictate that a Muslim is forbidden to harm the following categories of people during wartime: women, children, old people, non-combatants, those who surrender, trees or buildings (when it can be helped) and animals, nor can they torture, murder or mutilate those whom they capture, nor the bodies or tombs of the dead.

is attacked by a foreign power that is rebellious against God. In that case, it is the duty of every citizen to come forward for Jihad.

Given that Muslims are theoretically one community, regardless of artificial national borders, nearby Muslim countries are duty-bound to help their neighbors if they are in danger of being overwhelmed by an invading force. If this is still not enough to turn the tide of victory, then all the Muslims of the world must unite to fight the common foe. In these types of scenarios, Jihad becomes just as much a primary act of service to God as daily prayers and fasting in Ramadan. Whoever avoids this duty would be a sinner. His every claim to faith would be in doubt and hypocrisy would be the label he would find cast over him if he failed in this test of sincerity. In addition, all his other acts of service would be revealed as a sham, a worthless, hollow show of devotion.

# 6
# Faith and the Law of God

Thus far we've been discussing the concept of what living the lifestyle of Islam entails. Now we can begin a more thorough discussion of the framework of Divine Law, known as Shari'ah in Arabic. But let us first be clear about the difference between a lifestyle based on faith and the principles of living by the Divine Law, or Shari'ah.

## How are Faith and Law Related?

In an earlier chapter we noted that all of the prophets who were raised by God through the ages, and who appeared in various cultures all over the world, taught the same basic core message, i.e. Islam. This is a very fundamental point. They taught the principles of faith in God and His attributes, in the Day of Judgment, in the concept of prophets and in scriptural revelation. After imparting these teachings they then asked their people to live a life of obedience and submission to their Lord. This is what constitutes the lifestyle of faith, and it was a common theme found in the teachings of all of the prophets.

Apart from this spiritually-oriented lifestyle there is the Shari'ah, or the code of conduct, which gives the details about how to serve God, what is moral or immoral and the rules for living together in harmony. This body of what we might label as 'religious law' has been undergoing amendments throughout time as human civilization advanced and could handle more. Every prophet taught the same basic theological doctrines, but they each brought a different version of Divine Law, i.e. an individualized code that could suit the conditions of his own people and time.

This gradualist approach served the purpose of training different people through the ages and would (if the people listened) eventually lead their descendants to a more advanced level of civilization and equip them with a higher set of morals. This evolutionary process of imparting the law in segments over time ended with the advent of Muhammad, the last prophet, peace be upon him, who brought with him the final code which was to apply to all humanity for all times to come.

Muslim artisans often decorate everyday objects with verses from the Qur'an or sayings of the Prophet.

The basic doctrines of faith did not change, but now all the previous codes of religious law stand abrogated in view of the comprehensive Shari'ah that Muhammad, peace be upon him, had brought with him. This is the climax of the great process of training that was started at the dawn of humanity's existence.

## What are the Sources for God's Laws?

We draw upon two major textual sources in order to codify the Divine Law that Muhammad, peace be upon him, brought. These consist of two things: a book known as the Qur'an, which Muslims believe is the direct revelation of God. The other source is the collected sayings and pronouncements of Muhammad, which Muslims believe also reflects the teachings of God as expressed through the life example of His Prophet. This second source is known collectively as the Hadith, or Traditions.

The Qur'an is a divine revelation- each and every word of it is from God, but the Hadith is a collection of instructions issued by the last Prophet for how to understand and live by the broad principles espoused in the Qur'an. The Traditions also describe the Prophet's conduct, behavior and manners.

These and other details about the life and times of Muhammad, peace be upon him, were preserved by those who were present in his company or by those to whom these reports were handed down to in a chain of narration going back to the original eye-witness. These voluminous reports were later sifted, tested for authenticity and collected together by scholars who compiled them by topic into books. The most famous six collections are known simply by the name of the scholar who compiled each. They are (in order of importance): Bukhari, Muslim, At-Tirmidhi, Abu Dawud, An-Nisa'i and Ibn Majah.

## The Difference between the Qur'an and Hadith

The Qur'an is a book of revelation- a scripture, and thus takes on a regal tone and expresses broad themes that are applicable to anyone's life and understanding anywhere. The Hadith Traditions are the everyday teachings of Muhammad about Islam in his own words. They are not considered Divine revelation, but they are held as being words of merit and value as a true prophet, guided by God, uttered them.

The Qur'an, itself, tells believers to follow Muhammad's example and instructions. How do the two works compliment each other? For example, the Qur'an often exhorts Muslims to pray daily, but it does not give instructions on how to pray, or what sorts of things to say or even how to prepare oneself for a prayerful attitude. This is where Muhammad's detailed teaching come in. Below is an example of how the Qur'an and the sayings of Muhammad, peace be upon him, differ in tone and style.

# Comparing the Qur'an and Hadith

The Qur'an is a book of revelation- a scripture, and thus takes on a regal tone and expresses broad themes that are applicable to anyone's life and understanding anywhere. The Hadith Traditions are the everyday teachings of Muhammad about Islam in his own words. They are not considered Divine revelation, but they are held as being words of merit and value as a true prophet, guided by God, uttered them.

The Qur'an, itself, tells believers to follow Muhammad's example and instructions. How do the two works compliment each other? For example, the Qur'an often exhorts Muslims to pray daily, but it does not give instructions on how to pray, or what sorts of things to say or even how to prepare oneself for a prayerful attitude. This is where Muhammad's detailed teaching come in. Below is an example of how the Qur'an and the sayings of Muhammad, peace be upon him, differ in tone and style.

| The Qur'an | A Saying of the Prophet |
|---|---|
| "O you who believe, shall I lead you to a bargain that will save you from a painful doom? It is that you trust in God and in His Messenger and then strive in His cause with your wealth and your persons. That is the best for you if you only knew."<br><br>- Qur'an 61:10-11<br><br>- | "When you see someone who is better off than you, look at one who is not as well off as you. Doing this will keep you from despising the blessings that God has given to you."<br><br>- From the collection by Imam Muslim |

## Fiqh, or the Science of Law in Islam

Legal scholars all throughout Muslim history have exerted their utmost to find solutions to everyday problems utilizing the framework of the Qur'an and the Hadith literature. Thus modern believers owe a debt of gratitude to those talented men and women of the past whose vision and dedication, reflected in their mastery of the Qur'an and Hadith, made it easy for every Muslim to fashion his or her everyday affairs according to the requirements of the Shari'ah, or Divine Law. It's because of them that Muslims all over the world can follow the Shari'ah easily and efficiently without ever needing to delve too deeply into the interpretations and minute details involved in understanding the scope and breadth of Divine Law.

Indeed, in the early centuries of Islamic civilization there were many scholars involved in the work of systematizing and organizing the body of Divine Law into an easily understood and applicable lifestyle guide, over the years the works of these scholars and their unique positions, were gradually merged together until today where we find four major legal schools remaining. These legal schools differ in some minor details, but agree on almost everything else. Think of them as the complimentary studies of legal scholars whose aim is to make it easy for believers to pattern their life according to the principles of God's Laws. The four major (Sunni sect) schools are known by the name of their principle founder and are as follows:

- Hanafi: This is the legal tradition compiled by Abu Hanifa (700-767 CE) with the assistance and cooperation of many contemporary scholars and experts in Qur'anic and Traditional literature.

- Maliki: This school of thought was derived by Malik bin Anas (716-795 CE). He was the author of one of the earliest books on Divine Law.

- Shafi'i: A legal school founded by Muhammad al-Shafi'i (767-820 CE). He was the first to classify the sources of Islamic law as including both the Qur'an and Hadith as well as the opinions of the prophet's direct followers and independent reasoning.

- Hanbali: This school was founded by Ahmed bin Hanbal (780-855 CE).

All of these legal traditions, or schools, (which essentially codified the do's and don't's of Islam to make it easier for the common person to follow the Divine Law,) were given their final format within three hundred years of the time of the Prophet. Any differences that exist between the four schools are but the natural outcome of the fact that human understanding is a many sided thing. When different people employ themselves in interpreting a given body of knowledge, they will inevitably come up with different explanations according to their own level of skill, thought and understanding.

What gives these various schools of thought the authenticity that is associated with them is the unimpeachable integrity of their respective founders and the authenticity of the methods they adopted. That's why Muslims in general, no matter which school they may adhere to, regard all the four schools of law as equally valid. The consensus is that a person can follow any one of them and be rightly guided on the straight path for the rest of his life.

There is a movement in modern times, however, that promotes the idea that if a person acquires a certain level of competent knowledge in understanding the sources of Islam, then they can approach the Qur'an and Hadith literature unaided by the principles of traditional Islamic scholasticism and render judgments for themselves on what constitutes Divine Law.

## Mystical Dimensions of the Heart

The Islamic legal sciences (Fiqh) deal with the practical and physical fulfillment of Divine Law as applied to everyday life, but there is another dimension to Islamic practice, however, that deals with the spirit behind the letter of the law. This is known as *tasawwuf*, or the inner spiritual orientation. (In English it is known as Sufism.) For example, when we perform our daily ritual prayers, the law will judge us only by the fulfillment of the outward requirements such as making proper ablutions, facing towards the Ka'bah in Mecca, adhering to the timing and the number of movements within the prayer, etc., while *tasawwuf* judges the inner qualities of our prayers by our concentration, devotion, purity, sincerity and the effect (or lack of effect) that the prayers have upon our morals and manners.

Thus, true Islamic spirituality is the measure of our spirit of obedience and sincerity, while the legal side governs our carrying out of God's commands to the last detail. An act of service that is devoid of spirit, though correct in procedure, is like a good looking person who has a lousy personality, while an act of service that is full of spirit, but improperly performed, is like a wonderful person who just happens to suffer from a physical defect.

The above example makes clear the relationship between the letter of the law and the spirit of the law, but it is to the misfortune of Muslims that - as their civilization decreased in knowledge and strength (after the devastation of the Mongol invasions in the 13th century on through to European colonialism) - that they also succumbed to the misguided philosophies of the nations that dominated over them. Some misguided Muslims began to look for a "quick-fix" to their dilemma and began to "patch up" Islam with the faulty dogmas of foreign cultures, when it wasn't Islam that needed fixing, but our understanding of it.

They polluted the pure spring of Islamic *tasawwuf* with absurdities that could not be justified on the basis of the Qur'an and the Hadith, such as allowing the drinking of alcohol (which Islam forbids) or believing in saints that could give us favors from beyond the grave. Gradually a category of people arose who thought and proclaimed that they were immune to and above the requirements of the Shari'ah. (Thus, there is orthodox good Sufism and outlandish or unorthodox bad Sufism.)

This philosophy of anything goes as long as it seems spiritual is, of course, totally outside of the concept of Islam, for Islam cannot accept a spiritual tradition that is outside the bounds of God's Law- a law that applies to all creatures in the heavens and the earth. No seeker of mystical truth has the right to transgress the limits of the Shari'ah, or treat the primary obligations of faith such as daily prayers, fasting, charity, and the pilgrimage, as negotiable.

*Tasawwuf*, in the true sense, is nothing less than an intense love for God and His Prophet, Muhammad, peace be upon him, and such love requires a strict obedience to their commands as embodied in the Book of God and the life example of the Prophet. Anyone who deviates from following the commands of their Lord makes a false claim of love for God and His Messenger.

# 7

# How Does it All Fit Together?

Our discussion of the fundamentals of Islam would remain incomplete if we didn't present a grand overview of the way in which the law of Islam influences our lives both on the personal level as well as in society. This will help us to better visualize the type of person and community that Islam seeks to produce. In this chapter we will take a closer look into how the principles of Divine Law function on the practical level so that our overall conception of Islam can be complete, and also so that we can appreciate the validity and purpose of the Islamic way of life.

## Divine Law and You

People have been endowed with countless abilities and skills, and fortune has been very generous to us in this respect. We have intelligence and wisdom, a will to act and some measure of free choice. We also have the ability to see, speak, taste, touch and hear. We have the added benefit of strength, speed and agility, along with the powerful emotions of love, fear and anger. All of these facets of our being are useful to us, and none of them are unnecessary or extra. These abilities have been given to us because we need them desperately. They're indispensable to us for our survival. The life and success of every individual depends upon the proper use of these gifts, but on a higher level, we all must realize that they are tools given to us by God and are meant to be employed in His service, and unless they are exercised to their fullest potential, then the ultimate potential of our lives will have been wasted. God has also provided us with the means and resources which are needed to put our natural abilities to use and to achieve the fulfillment of our needs. Indeed, the human body has been designed to be our greatest tool in our struggle to survive in the shifting fortunes of unbridled nature.

Then there is the world in which we live. Our environment and surroundings contain resources of every description; resources which we use to achieve our objectives. The environment, and all that is within it, has been harnessed for us and we can make every conceivable use of it. We also have fellow creatures of our own species- our fellow men and women- who are there so that we can cooperate with each other in the construction of a better and more prosperous world.

Now reflect deeply upon this interplay of so many forces. These powers and resources have been given to you so they can be used for the good of others. They have been created for your good and are not meant to harm or destroy you. Their function is to enrich our lives with the good and the pure and not to throw us into jeopardy. Thus, the proper use of these abilities is to use them in whatever way that benefits us, and the most beneficial thing of all is to please God and reach out to our fellow creatures in peace and harmony.

Even if there might be some risks involved in what we must do to survive in this world, for example, weathering the hazards of nature or negotiating the unforeseen consequences of accidents and the like, they must be managed and weighed as carefully as they can be. If a person lives their life at this level (trying to do right, trying to be all that he can be, and then not being afraid to take occasional chances,) it would be enough proof that he is doing what he is supposed to do with the endowments he has been given.

On the flip side, any action that results in waste and meaningless destruction is simply wrong, unreasonable and uncalled for. Nature itself wastes nothing and it is the grandest design of our Creator. If you do something that causes destruction or injury, it would be a mistake, pure and simple. Further still, if your actions hurt others and make you a nuisance to them, it would not only be foolishness, it would be a total misuse of your God-given powers. Such actions are flagrantly unreasonable, for it is human reason itself that demands that destruction and injury must be avoided and that the path of gain and progress be pursued. Any deviation from this mindset of growth and good management is a sign of misdirection.

Keeping this in mind, when we look at human beings, we find there are two kinds of people. First, there are those who knowingly misuse the skills that God gave them, and through this misuse they waste their resources, injure their own vital interests, and hurt other people. Then there are those who are sincere and earnest but who make mistakes out of ignorance. Those who intentionally misuse their abilities are wicked, they generate evil and they deserve the consequences of the long arm of the law to keep them in check. Those who slip up on account of ignorance need knowledge and guidance so they can learn to see the right path and make the best use of their skills. It is this system of checks and balances- based wholly upon Divine Law-which God revealed to humanity that fulfills this very need.

Divine Law makes God's regulations very clear and specific and thus provides guidance for how we should live. Its objective is to show us the best way to do something and it provides us with the principles to fulfill our needs in the most successful and beneficial way. The Law of God is a system of principles that are for our own good. Nothing in it leads you to waste your talents or suppresses your lawful passions and desires. Nothing in it seeks to obliterate your normal urges and emotions. It doesn't ask you to go and live like a hermit. It doesn't say, "Abandon the world, give up all ease and comfort, leave your homes and wander around in deserts, mountains and jungles, without bread or clothes, putting yourself through inconveniences and self-denial."

No, certainly not. This kind of thinking has no relevance in Islam, for Islam is the system created by the All-Knowing God for the ultimate benefit of humanity. Its laws are created by that very Being Who harnessed everything for our use. He would never wish to ruin or stifle His creation.

He hasn't given people any ability or urge that is useless, nor has He created anything in the entire universe which is useless to us. Rather, it's His expressed will that the universe- this grand workshop with its diversified activities- should go on functioning smoothly so that humanity- the prize of His creation- can make the most productive use of its potential. It is God's will that people should use everything provided for them on the earth and in space. They should use them in a way that allows them to reap the benefits all together. They should never intentionally or carelessly harm any of God's creation. Divine Law was made to guide our footsteps in this respect. It forbids all that is harmful to us, and allows all that is useful and beneficial to us.

What this law basically says is that people have the right, and in some cases the absolute duty, to fulfill all their genuine needs and desires. They should make every conceivable effort to promote their interests and achieve success and happiness. But, and it is an important but, they should do all this in such a way that the interests of others are not jeopardized. No harm should befall their fellow creatures as they work towards their own goals. All possible social cohesion, assistance, and cooperation should be accomplished in the achievement of their objectives.

Of course, there are some circumstances in which good and evil or gain and loss are irreversibly bound together. The attitude of the Divine Law in relation to this is to accept a little harm for the sake of gaining greater benefits. It also allows for the sacrifice of some benefit to avoid greater harm. This is the basic approach of the Divine Law in all fields of life.

Now we know that humanity's knowledge is limited. Most people throughout history have had a hard time knowing what is good and what is evil, what is helpful and what is harmful. The sources of human knowledge are too limited to provide us with crystal clear distinctions. That's why God revealed His principles for life and living which are absolutely correct and encompass a complete system for the entire human race to follow. The merits and truths of this system are becoming more apparent with the passage of time. Just a few centuries ago many of its advantages were hidden to the eye. They've now become crystal clear after the great leaps in philosophy, law and sociology that our civilization has made recently.

Even today, many people don't appreciate all the benefits of this system. But as knowledge progresses, new light is gained and it brings the superiority of a single, all encompassing code of conduct for all people to follow into greater perspective. The world has no choice but to drift toward the Divine system, even as nature has no choice but to function in accordance with the Divine Will. Although some political theories have emphasized the complete abandonment of religious

214

ideals, like Communism, what we have found is that Communism has failed, and once more laws, with roots in Divine revelation, are being incorporated into national and international charters at an ever increasing rate. Those who denied the truth of Divine revelation, and pinned all their hopes on unguided reason, after committing blunders and courting bitter experience, are adopting in one way or another the rules of Divine Law. But at what a cost! And even then, they're not using it in its entirety.

---

**Someone once asked Muhammad, peace be upon him, "What is faith?"**

**The Prophet replied, "When doing good makes you feel pleasure and doing wrong makes you feel terrible, then you are a believer."**

**Then the man asked, "What is a sin?"**

**The Prophet replied: "When something bothers your conscience, give it up."**

---

In contrast, there are people who put their trust in God's Prophets, and they accept what they taught, and adopt the Divine Law that they brought. They may not be aware of all the benefits of this or that instruction, but on the whole, they accept the code which is the outcome of true knowledge. They accept this system of laws which saves them from the evils and blunders of ignorance. They put their trust in the system of truth, rather than placing their hopes on trial and error. Such are the people who are on the right track and are bound to succeed.

## Balancing Rights and Obligations

The web of life which Islam envisions consists of an interconnected set of rights and obligations. Broadly speaking, the law of Islam imposes four kinds of rights and obligations on every man and woman. These are:

1. The rights of God upon us.
2. A person's rights upon his or herself.
3. Communal rights over individual rights.
4. The rights of nature which God has put at humanity's service.

This descending order of rights and obligations forms a very important part of Islam. It's the duty of every true Muslim to understand their significance and earnestly put them into practice. All of them have been discussed clearly and in detail within the canon of Divine Law. The method by which these obligations can be discharged is also provided. This is so that all of them can be put into practice at the same time, and none of them gets violated or left by the wayside. We will take a brief look at each of these rights and obligations so that an idea of the Islamic system of life can be formed.

## What are God's Rights?

First we must study the grounds upon which Islam bases the relationship of the individual to his or her Creator. The most important right that God has upon us is that all of us should have faith in Him alone. We should acknowledge His authority and associate none with Him. This is epitomized in the statement: *La elaha ill Allah* (there is no other god but the God).

The second right that God has upon us is that we must accept, without question, and follow His guidance- the system He revealed to humanity- and seek His pleasure with all the energy we have. We fulfill this right by believing in His Prophet and by accepting his guidance and teachings. The third right that He has upon us is that we must obey Him with complete honesty and without hesitation. We fulfill this obligation by following God's law as contained in the Qur'an and the teachings of the Prophet. The fourth right He has upon us is that we should serve Him. This is done through the various acts of service discussed earlier.

These important duties supersede all other rights and, as such, they must be performed even at the cost of some of the other lesser rights and duties. For example, in performing our daily ritual prayers, or in fasting, we must sacrifice many personal rights. A person has to undergo hardships and sacrifices when correctly performing his duties to his Creator. He has to get up early in the morning for prayer, and so must sacrifice his rest and sleep. During the day, he often puts off many important activities and gives some of his time just to pray to his Maker. In the month of fasting, he embraces hunger and puts up with many inconveniences just to please his Lord. By paying the required annual charity, he loses some of his wealth and demonstrates that the love of God is over and above everything else, and that the love of wealth cannot stand in its way. For pilgrimage, he undergoes sacrifices of wealth and bears the hardship of travel. And in jihad, he sacrifices money, material - all that he has- down to his very life.

When it comes to the rights of God, fulfilling your duty may mean that others lose some of their rights. You, too, may have some of your interests hurt. A worker has to leave his or her task when the time for prayer arrives in order to attend to the service of his or her Lord. A businessperson must interrupt his or her business engagements long enough to undertake the pilgrimage to Mecca. In jihad, a striving person may take away a life or give his own solely in the cause of God.

The rights that God has upon us make us sacrifice many things which we have (temporarily) in our control like wealth, time and resources. But the way that the infinitely wise God has constructed Divine Law ensures that any sacrifice of the rights of others has been reduced to the barest minimum. In addition, God has granted us a great deal of leeway so that we can easily fulfill the rights He has upon us. Look at the flexibility He's given to us so we can fulfill the obligation of prayer. If no water is available for ablution, you can merely pat your hands on clean sand and pass them over your face and arms to symbolically cleanse yourself. If you're traveling, you can shorten the duration of the prayers. If you're ill and can't stand up in prayer, you can perform it while sitting, and if you're too sick to sit, you can pray lying down.

An old mosque in present-day Bulgaria that combines elements of European and Turkish architecture. The mosque is as important to Muslims as churches and synagogues are to Christians and Jews.

Fasting follows the same principle of flexibility. If you're traveling or are sick, you don't have to fast and can make up any missed days at a more convenient time. Women are exempted from fasting if they're pregnant, during their menstrual periods, or during lactation. The fast must be broken at the appointed time, and without any delay. Any delay is disapproved of. You're allowed to eat and drink from sunset to the break of dawn every day. Optional fasts are highly valued by God, and He's pleased with them, but He doesn't want you to fast all the time and become too weak to adequately perform your ordinary duties like hold a job or raise a family.

Now look at the case of the annual charity (*zakat*); only the minimum rate has been fixed by God and people are left to freely give as much as they like beyond that in the cause of God. If the minimum amount is given, the basic duty is fulfilled. But if more is spent in charity, it shows that the person is seeking even more of God's pleasure. But here again He doesn't want us to sacrifice all that we own to charity, nor are we to deny ourselves or our relatives the rightful pleasures and comforts of life. He doesn't want us to impoverish ourselves, so we're commanded to be moderate when we donate to charity.

Then look at the institution of pilgrimage. Only those who are physically or financially able are required to perform it. The poor health of some and the impoverished conditions of others simply won't allow them to perform it. God understands these problems and in His mercy makes an exception for such people.

For those capable of it, it's only required once in a lifetime, and this in any year that is convenient. If there is a war or any other situation such as drought or bad weather which poses a risk to life, the Hajj can be postponed. Moreover, if your parents are very old you have to ask for their permission to go on the pilgrimage so that in their declining years they won't have to suffer any discomfort from your absence. All of these things clearly show the importance that God Almighty has given to the rights of others in contrast to His own rights.

The greatest sacrifice made in the way of God is jihad, or struggling in His cause. In it men and women sacrifice not only their own lives and belongings, but may have to destroy those of others as well. But the Islamic principle is that we should suffer a lesser loss in order to save ourselves from a greater one. What comparison would the loss of some lives - even if it were in the thousands or more- be to the disaster that would befall humanity as a result of the victory of evil over good. What comparison would it be to the tremendous anguish humanity would suffer if falsehood overtook truth, and if aggressive atheism won over the religion of God.

Not only would the religion of God be pushed aside, but the world would become the abode of evil, corruption, and perversion. Life would be disrupted from within and without. In order to prevent this greater evil, God has commanded us to sacrifice our lives and property for His cause. Yet He's forbidden unnecessary

221

bloodshed. Women, children, civilians, the crippled, the old, the sick and the wounded should under no circumstances be harmed. We would be guilty of a tremendous sin if we injured them. His order is to fight only those who rise to fight us.

God tells us not to cause unnecessary destruction of even the enemy's lands. Trees are not to be cut down, crops are not to be burnt, and homes are not to be looted and destroyed. The defeated must be dealt with fairly and honorably. We are instructed to observe any treaties made with the enemy and we must stop fighting when they ask for peace. We're not allowed to fight them any longer once they stop their aggressive and offensive activities. Thus Islam allows for only the minimum sacrifice of life, property, and the rights of others during the performance of the rights of God.

## What are Our Rights?

Next we have our own personal rights as human beings, i.e. the rights each individual has upon his or herself. The fact is, people are more cruel and unjust to themselves than to any other creature. On the surface it seems astonishing. How can people be the most unjust to themselves? How can they be their own worst enemy? It doesn't seem to make sense. But deeper reflection shows that it contains a large element of truth.

The greatest weakness that we have is this: when we're confronted by an overpowering desire, instead of resisting it, we often succumb to it. Then, in its gratification, we knowingly bring great harm upon ourselves. There are those who take to drinking; they become addicted to it and continue indulging in it at the cost of wasted money, ill-health, a damaged reputation, and the eventual loss of everything they might have.

Another person may be so fond of eating that he overeats to the point of spoiling his health and endangering his life. Yet another becomes a slave to his sexual appetites and ruins himself in over-indulgence. Still another gets tired of life and withdraws from everything. He suppresses his genuine desires and refuses to fulfill his natural physical requirements. Doing away with food, clothing, and shelter, he leaves his home and retreats into the mountains and forests. He believes the world is not meant for him and he hates everything in it. These are just a few examples of humanity's tendency to go to extremes and get lost.

Islam stands for the welfare of humanity and its avowed objective is to establish a balanced life, a life which follows a middle road. Islam wants to avoid the kind of life which follows the extremes at either end. This is why the Divine Law clearly declares that your own self has certain rights over you.

This law forbids the use of all things which injure our physical, mental, or moral existence. It forbids drinking blood or intoxicating drinks. We're told not to eat unclean animals; pork, beasts of prey, poisonous animals, and carcasses are banned. The main reason for food restrictions is that there are some substances that really have harmful effects upon the physical, moral, and intellectual life of the individual.

Even while forbidding these kinds of things, Islam allows people to use and enjoy everything that's clean, healthy and useful. Islam tells us not to deprive our bodies of wholesome food, for our bodies have a right upon us. Islam forbids nudity and orders us to wear decent and dignified clothing. It demands that we work for a living. It disapproves of laziness and makes it clear that the Muslim who works hard to earn his living is better than the one who does little and earns nothing. The true message of Divine Law is that people should use both the abilities that God has given them, and the resources that He has spread throughout the world, for their comfort and welfare.

Islam doesn't believe in the suppression of sexual desires. It tells people to regulate these desires by seeking their fulfillment through marriage. It forbids people from persecuting themselves, from denying themselves the rightful comforts and pleasures of life. To become elevated spiritually, or to seek nearness to God, it isn't necessary to abandon this world. To achieve salvation in the next life, there's no need to negate the life of this world. Instead, the true trial of life lies within this world, remaining in its midst and following the Divine system here in this world. The road to success lies squarely in adhering to the principles of Divine Law in the midst of life's complexities -and not outside of it.

Islam absolutely forbids suicide and impresses upon us that life belongs to God. It's like a trust which God has bestowed upon us for a certain period of time. He gave life to each individual so he or she could make the best use of it- it's not meant to be spoiled and destroyed in a foolish act of desperation. Suicide is the most outrageous and ridiculous manifestation of people neglecting the rights of their own selves.

## What Do We Owe to Others?

Even though Divine Law has told us to fulfill our personal needs, we must not seek their fulfillment in such a way that the rights of others are violated. Divine Law seeks to strike a balance between the rights of individuals and the rights of society. This is so that no conflict will arise between the two, and both will cooperate in establishing the law of God.

Islam strongly forbids the telling of a lie, for it defiles the liar, harms other people, and is a source of menace to society. It has totally forbidden theft, bribery, forgery, cheating and interest on investments. The reason for this is because whatever people gain by these means is really obtained by causing loss and injury to others. Backbiting, lying, slandering, maligning, gambling, lottery, speculation and all games of chance have been prohibited, for in all of them one gains at the cost of others losing.

All forms of exploitation in commerce, where one party alone is the winner, have been prohibited. Resource hoarding, black-marketeering, withholding of land from cultivation and all other forms of individual and social aggrandizement have been outlawed. Murder, debauchery, the spreading of mischief, disorder, and vandalism have been made crimes. They're illegal because no one has the right to take away the life and property of another just so he can gain some personal gratification. Adultery, fornication and unnatural sexual indulgences have been strictly prohibited as well.

It's common knowledge that these practices not only violate morality and impair the health of their perpetrator, but they also spread corruption and immorality in society. They cause venereal diseases (STDs) and ruin public health. This leads to the degeneration of the health and morals of future generations. Human relationships are severed, and the very fabric of the cultural and social structure of the community is destroyed. Islam wants to eliminate even the slightest possibility of such a dismal outcome.

Each of these limits has been imposed upon us by Islam to prevent us from encroaching upon the rights of others. Islam doesn't want people to become so selfish and egotistical that they shamelessly abuse the rights of others, and violate all standards of decency, simply for the attainment of a few monetary gains or physical pleasures. Nor does it allow people to crucify the interests of others in order to gain more personal benefits for themselves.

Islamic law regulates life so succinctly in order to ensure that the welfare of every individual is protected. But for the sake of the overall welfare and cultural advancement of humanity as a whole, a few personal restrictions are not enough. In a truly peaceful and prosperous society, it's not enough that there are regulations to stop people from violating the rights of others. Indeed, it's also necessary that people work together in social institutions which contribute towards the welfare of all. Only through communal effort can people ever hope to establish an ideal society. Divine Law guides us in this respect as well. Here is a brief summary of those communal aspects of Islamic Law which seek to create a just society for all.

The family is the cradle of the human being. Here is where our most important characteristics are built. For this reason, it's not only the cradle of each individual, but the cradle of civilization as well. Divine Law contains specific rules concerning the family. A family consists of a husband, a wife, and their children. The rules concerning the family are very explicit. The man is assigned the responsibility of earning and providing the necessities of life for his wife and children. He must protect them from all the difficulties and problems of life. The woman is assigned the duty of managing the household. Here she must train and bring up the children in the best possible way. She must also provide her husband and children with the greatest love and comfort she can. As for the children, it's their duty to respect and obey their parents and, when they're grown, to serve them and provide for their needs. In order to make the household a well-managed and disciplined institution, Islam has adopted the following measures:

- The husband has been made the head of the family. No institution can work smoothly unless there is a chief administrator in it. To have a school without a principal or a city without a mayor is unthinkable. If there's no one in charge of an institution, nothing but chaos will result. If every person in a family went his or her own way, nothing but confusion would prevail. If the husband goes in one direction and the wife in another, the future psychological well-being of the children would be in jeopardy. There must be someone serving as the head of the family so that family cohesion is maintained. In this way, the family can become the model for the ideal institution of society. By giving this position to the husband, Islam makes the family a disciplined primary unit of an overall disciplined civilization. The family is a model for society as a whole.

- This head of the family has further been burdened with other responsibilities. It's his duty to earn a living, and to carry out those tasks which are performed outside the household. It has freed all women from extra household duties and placed them all upon the shoulders of the husband. Women have been relieved from having to perform tasks outside the house so that they can devote themselves to what happens in the home. The reason is that now they can focus all their energies on the maintenance of the household and the rearing of children, (who are the future citizens and parents of the nation.) Islam doesn't want women to have to do double or triple the work: to rear children, maintain the household, earn a living, and do outside jobs. This, Islam believes, is asking too much of them. That obviously would be an injustice. Islam, therefore, produces a functional distribution of work between the sexes.

But this doesn't mean that women aren't allowed to go out of the house. This is not the case at all! Women are allowed to go out whenever necessary, and even to hold a job if they like (the only caveat being that they shouldn't sacrifice their home life and children for the sake of a career). The law has specified the home as their primary field of responsibility, and has stressed the great value attained if women attend to the maintenance of their household.

The general concept of family in Islam is that the size of the family widens through the addition of relatives and marriage connections. To bind together the members of the family into one unit, to keep their relations close and healthy, and to make each of them a source of support, strength and contentment to the other, Islam has provided certain basic family values. These values may be summed up as follows:

*1. Who we can and cannot marry has been clearly defined: The relationships where marriage is forbidden are: mother and son, father and daughter, step-father and step-daughter, stepmother and step-son, brother and sister, foster brother and foster sister, an uncle and his niece, an aunt and her nephew, mother-in-law and son-in-law, and father-in-law and daughter-in-law. This prohibition strengthens the bonds of the family and makes relations between these relatives absolutely pure. They can mix with each other without restraint and with sincere affection.*

*2. Beyond the limits of the forbidden marriages, matrimonial relations can occur between members of related families or clans so as to bind them still closer. Marriage connections between families which are freely associated with each other, and which therefore know each other's habits, customs, and traditions, are generally successful. Therefore, Divine Law permits.*

*3. In a group of related families, there usually coexists both the rich and the poor, the prosperous and the destitute. The Islamic principle is that a person's relatives have the greatest right upon him. There is great respect for the ties between relatives. Muslims must respect this bond in every possible way. To be disloyal to one's relatives and to be negligent of their rights is a great sin, and God has disapproved of it. If a relative becomes poor, or is beset with trouble, it's the duty of his rich and prosperous relatives to help him. In giving zakat and other charity, special regard for the rights of relatives has been enjoined.*

*4. The law of inheritance is so constructed in Islam that the property left by the deceased cannot become concentrated in any one place. It's distributed in a way that allows all close relatives to get their share. Sons, daughters, wives, husbands, fathers, mothers, brothers, and sisters are the nearest and their share in inheritance comes first. If none of that category of relatives exists, shares are given to the next nearest relatives. Therefore, after a person dies, his or her wealth is distributed among their relatives, and a fatal blow is struck at the capitalistic concept of the absolute concentration of wealth.*

The law of Islam is uniquely excellent, and other nations are now taking note of its principles. (The sad irony is that some Muslims themselves are not fully aware of its revolutionary potential and, in ignorance, many of them are not putting it into practice. For example, in several parts of the Muslim world, daughters are routinely deprived of their share of an inheritance. This is a clear injustice and a flagrant violation of the Qur'an's clear guidelines on this matter.)

After the familial level, our relations with our friends, neighbors, fellow-citizens, and people with whom we come into constant contact is examined by Islam. Islam recognizes these relationships and tells a Muslim to treat them all honestly, equitably, and courteously. It tells the believers to be careful not to hurt others' feelings, to avoid indecent and abusive language, and to help each other. We are to take care of the sick, support the poor, and assist the needy and the crippled. We must also sympathize with the people stricken by trouble or disaster. We must look after orphans and widows, feed the hungry, cloth the ragged and help the unemployed in seeking employment as well.

Islam says that if God has given you wealth and riches, then you must not squander it on luxurious frivolities. It has prohibited the use of gold and silver dishes, costly silken clothes (for men), and wasting money on useless ventures and extravagant luxuries.

These injunctions of Divine Law are based upon the principle that no one should be allowed to squander upon himself wealth that can maintain thousands of human beings. It's cruel and unjust that money which can be used to feed the starving be tossed away in useless or extravagant decorations, exhibitions, or expensive baubles and belongings. What one has earned or inherited is beyond a doubt his own property. Islam recognizes this right and allows him to enjoy it and make the best use of it. It also suggests that if you are wealthy, you should have better clothes, better housing, and a more decent living. But Islam wants to make sure that in all of our activities, the humane element is not lost sight of.

What Islam totally disapproves of is conceited self-centeredness. It disapproves of egotistical thinking which leads to neglecting the welfare of others and gives birth to exaggerated individualism. It wants the entire society to prosper, not merely a few stray individuals. It instills in the minds of its followers social consciousness and suggests they lead a simple and sparing life. They should avoid excess and waste in every aspect of life and strive to follow a middle road. They can fulfill their just needs, while keeping in mind the needs of others. Again, the rich shouldn't neglect the needs of their fellow-citizens but rather should treat them as if they were their brothers and sisters. This is the sense of human equality that Islam wants to achieve.

So far, we've discussed the nature of our relationship with our more immediate circles. Now let's look at the wider perspective and see what kind of community Islam wants to establish. Anyone who embraces Islam not only enters the fold of the religion, but also becomes a member of the Islamic community. Divine Law contains certain rules of behavior for relationships on this higher level as well. These rules assure that all people work together and help each other to perform what is good, and they also have the added function of forbidding what's harmful and evil in society. Rules, then, are set up to make sure that no sinfulness can creep into our society, and if some by chance does, the rules provide ways to eliminate it. Some of these rules are as follows:

1. *To preserve the moral life of the nation, and to ensure that the society evolves along healthy lines, unregulated mingling of the sexes has been prohibited. Islam wants there to be a functional division between the sexes. It provides different spheres of activity for both of them. Outside the limits of the nearest relatives between whom marriage is forbidden, men and women have been asked not to mix randomly with each other, and when they do come into contact with each other (in the stores, at school, or on the street) they should conduct themselves with proper manners and be dressed conservatively. When men or women leave their homes, they should wear plain clothing and be dressed modestly.*

*Along with this, men and women have been asked not to stare longingly at each other. Instead, they should keep their eyes lowered and avoid gawking. If someone accidentally happens to stare at someone from the opposite sex, then they are advised to avert their glance. To stare at someone from the opposite sex whom we are not married to or related to is wrong and further still, to try and set up secret meetings is worse. It's the duty of both men and women to look after their personal morality and to purge their souls of all impurities. Marriage is the proper forum for intimate relationships, and no one should attempt to overstep this boundary, or even hint at any concept of 'sexual freedom' which is really sexual anarchy. Our minds should be completely cleansed from such perverse ideas.*

*2. People are encouraged to wear decent and respectable dress. No man should expose his body from the knees to the navel, nor should a woman expose any part of her body except her face, hands and feet to anyone other than her husband. To keep these parts covered is the religious duty of every man and woman. Through this directive, Islam wants to cultivate in its followers a deep sense of modesty and purity. It wants to suppress all forms of immodesty, lewdness and moral deviation.*

*3. Islam doesn't approve of pastimes, entertainment or diversions that can stimulate sensual passions. It doesn't respect things which weaken and corrupt the principles of morality. Such pastimes are a sheer waste of time, money, and energy, and they can destroy the moral backbone of society. Recreation in itself is no doubt a necessity. It acts* as a spur to activity and quickens the spirit of life and adventure. It's as important to life as water and air. Nothing is more satisfying than to enjoy recreational activities after a hard day's work. But recreation must be of the type that refreshes the mind and enlivens the spirit, not of the sort which depresses the soul and incites the passions. The absurd and wasteful spectacles where thousands of people witness awful scenes of violence and sexual immorality (such as at music concerts or boxing matches) are the exact opposite of healthy recreation. Although they may satisfy the senses and excite the passions, their effects upon the minds and morals of the people is horrifying. These poor excuses for entertainment spoil our habits and morals and have no place in an Islamic society. Its culture wants nothing to do with such crude and corrupting practices.

4. To safeguard the strong bond of unity and the solidarity of the nation, and to achieve a state of well-being for all within the community, the faithful have been told to avoid mutual hostility and social dissension. Sectarianism of every type has been made totally forbidden. Islam came precisely to cleanse the earth of such corrupt practices which divide people into separate groups on the basis of language, race, color or culture. Those within the Islamic community who segregate themselves based on any of these categories are committing a great crime against the religion of God.

If, as is inevitable, differences do arise, Muslims have been told to settle any disputes according to the principles laid down in the Qur'an and the Sunnah, or life example of

235

*the Prophet Muhammad, peace be upon him. If the parties fail to reach a settlement, instead of fighting and quarreling amongst themselves, they should try to coexist with their differences in the name of God and leave the decision to Him. In matters of national concern, they should help each other for the sake of progress. Quarreling and bickering over trivial things should be avoided as a waste of useful time and energy. Such conflicts and schisms are a disgrace to the Muslim community and a potential source of national weakness. They must be shunned at all costs.*

*5. Islam regards science and technology as the common property of humanity. Islam demands that its followers seek knowledge and explore the sciences, for knowledge is the key to success. Muslims have full liberty to learn about them and use them in whatever way they can. But the same does not apply to the issue of culture and lifestyle. Muslims are forbidden from imitating the ways of life of other nations. The psychology of imitation suggests that it springs from a sense of inferiority and its net result is the cultivation of a defeatist mentality.*

Cultural copying has extremely negative effects upon a nation. It destroys its inner vitality, blurs its vision, and clouds its skills. Breeding a national inferiority complex, it gradually but assuredly saps the very spirit of the culture and its identity. It literally sounds its death bell. This is why Muhammad, peace be upon him, clearly and forcefully forbade Muslims from adopting the culture and lifestyle of non-Muslims. The strength of a nation doesn't lie in its dress, manners, or fine arts, rather its growth and strength rests in having correct knowledge and helpful scientific advancements. It's a result of the nation's ability to discipline itself, and to use knowledge and technical accomplishments for the betterment of humanity, while rejecting those arts and crafts which breed cultural slavery.

With these issues behind us, we can now come to a discussion about the types of relations which Muslims are supposed to have with non-Muslims. In dealing with them, the believers are instructed not to be intolerant or narrow-minded. They have been told not to abuse or speak ill of their religious leaders or saints, nor say anything insulting about their religion. They must not seek disagreements with them without reason, but are to live in peace and harmony. If non-Muslims observe a peaceful and conciliatory attitude towards Muslims, and don't violate their territories, or violate the rights of others, then Muslims should keep cordial relations with them. They should be dealt with fairly and justly.

It's the very dictate of our religion that we must strive to possess greater human sympathy and politeness than any other people. We must behave in the most noble and modest way. Bad manners, oppression, arrogance, aggression, and bigotry run counter to the inner spirit of Islam. A Muslim is born in this world to become a living symbol of goodness, nobility and humanity. He should impress people by his character and example. Only then can he become a true ambassador of the way of life known as submission to God, i.e. Islam.

# Animal Rights in Islam

Now we come to the last category of rights, that of the rights of the creatures who have been placed under our control. God has honored humanity with authority over His countless creatures. Everything has been harnessed for his use. People have the power to subdue the various creatures of the world and make them serve their purposes. This superior position gives us the authority to literally use them as we like. But this doesn't mean that God has allowed us to go unchecked in our use of the plants and animals of the earth. Humanity has not been given complete liberty to use the natural world just any old way.

Islam says that all of creation has certain rights upon humanity. First and foremost, people shouldn't waste natural resources or living creatures on fruitless ventures, nor should they hurt or destroy them unnecessarily. When people use animals to serve them, they should cause them the least possible harm. The Islamic system contains many examples of these rights. We are allowed, for instance, to slaughter animals for food, but we've been forbidden to kill them merely for fun or sport. By this, we would be depriving them of their lives unnecessarily, and this is a criminal act. In killing them for food, a humane method of slaughtering has been dictated, and it's the best possible method for doing so. Other methods currently in use among the peoples of the world are either more painful or spoil the meat, depriving it of some of its useful properties.

Islam avoids both of these problems and suggests a method which, on the one hand, causes the animal little to no pain, and on the other, preserves the healthy and useful properties of the meat. Killing an animal by subjecting it to continuous pain and injury is considered abominable in Islam. Islam allows the killing of dangerous and venomous animals and beasts of prey only because it values a human's life more than theirs. But here too, it doesn't allow their killing through prolonged, painful methods.

Regarding beasts of burden and those used for transportation, Islam forbids people from keeping them hungry, expecting hard and intolerable work from them, or beating them cruelly. To catch birds and imprison them without any special purpose is considered shameful. Moving beyond animals, Islam doesn't approve of the useless cutting of trees and bushes. People can use their fruits and produce, but they have no right to destroy them without warrant. Plants, after all, are alive.

Islam doesn't allow the waste of even lifeless things. Its attitude of conservation is so firm that it strongly disapproves of even wasting water when water is abundant. Islam's avowed objective is to avoid waste in every conceivable form and to make the best possible use of all resources, whether animate or inanimate, living or lifeless.

## Shari'ah: the Divine Law

We have attempted to offer a brief summary of Islamic law, the law which prophet Muhammad, peace be upon him, delivered to humanity for all times to come. This law doesn't accept artificial difference between people, and instead holds to the proposition that it is only in belief and moral action that one can say there are superior or inferior people. Those religions and social systems, and those political and cultural ideologies which make classifications among people on the grounds of race, country, or color can never become universal systems.

The simple reason is that a person who belongs to a certain race cannot be transformed into another race, nor can a person born in a certain country ever completely absolve himself from identification with that place. Neither can the world, under such systems, merge together into one country, as the color of a black, white or yellow person cannot be changed.

Such systems and ideologies must remain confined to one race, one country, or one community. They're bound to be narrow, limited, and nationalistic, for this reason they can never become universal. Islam, on the other hand, is a universal system. Anyone who declares belief in the concept that "there is no god worthy of worship except Almighty God, and that Muhammad is His last and universal Messenger" enters the fold of Islam and is entitled to the same rights as all other Muslims.

This is a revolutionary concept. It says that in an Islamic society, a Persian, an Arab, an African or an American could be the leader of the nation, for the factor of eligibility as head of state would only be his commitment to God. The same would be true for a black, white or a oriental man. Someone could be an immigrant, or of an entirely different race or nationality than the governing majority, yet he could still become the ruler of the nation. This only rarely ever occurs in the national systems of today.

One has difficulty imagining even now a member of an extreme minority becoming the leader of a major country in which he is a racial or ethnic minority. And it is nearly impossible for an immigrant to even hope to become a parliamentarian or congressman, let alone stand for the highest offices in the land.

Yet there is another revolutionary result of this simple statement of God's supremacy. It raises humanity to the highest levels of thought and conception, for through it they recognize their rightful direction and purpose in life. They can invoke upon themselves the tremendous and immeasurable blessings and rewards of Almighty God. Humanity gains these blessings because the realization and implementation of this statement invokes the pleasure of God, the Most Great. Nothing in life could be greater than that.

Islam is not a 'religion' in the sense that this word is commonly understood. It's a system encompassing all fields of life. Islam touches upon politics, economics, legislation, science, the humanities, health, psychology and sociology. It's a system which makes no discrimination on the basis of race, color, language or any other external categories. Its appeal is to all the people of the world. It wants to touch the heart of every human being no matter who they are or where they come from.

This system of law is also eternal. It's not based upon the customs or traditions of any particular people, and is not meant for a specific period of history. It's based on the same principles of nature upon which humanity was created, and since this nature remains the same in all times and under all circumstances, and since this nature cannot be changed, the law based upon its principles is applicable to all ages. This universal and eternal religion is Islam.

## In Conclusion

The purpose of this book is to offer all those Muslims and non-Muslims, who have little or no access to the original sources of Islam, a brief but comprehensive overview of Islam. We've tried to avoid overloading our discussion with technical details, and have instead attempted to portray the entire worldview of Islam in one sweeping narrative. We haven't limited the scope of this book to merely stating what Muslims believe in or stand for, because we've also attempted to explain the rational foundations for these beliefs. Similarly, we didn't limit ourselves to only introducing the Islamic methods of serving and worshipping God, but rather have also tried to unveil the wisdom behind them. It's our hope that this brief summary will go a long way towards satisfying the intellectual cravings of today's young people, and will help non-Muslims in understanding what Islam is all about.

# Resources for Further Study

## Books

A Journey through the Holy Qur'an.
Translated by Yahiya Emerick. Available
from www.ifna.net

Understanding the Qur'an: Themes and Styles. By
Muhammad Abdel Haleem. I.B. Taurus, 2001.

The Life and Work of Muhammad. By
Yahiya Emerick. Alpha Books, Indianapolis,
2002.

Imam Bukhari's Book of Muslim Morals
and Manners. Translated by Yusuf Talal De
Lorenzo. Al-Saadawi Publications,
Herndon, 1997.

The Complete Idiot's Guide to
Understanding Islam. By Yahiya Emerick.
Alpha Books, Indianapolis, 2004.

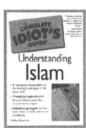

The Bible, the Qur'an and Science. By Maurice Bucaille.
Tahrike Tarsile Qur'an, New York, 2001.

An Islamic Treasury of Virtues. By Wahiduddin Khan.
Goodwordbooks, New Delphi, 1998.

No god but God. By Reza Aslan. Random House, 2005.

The Complete Idiot's Guide to Rumi Meditation. By
Yahiya Emerick. Alpha Books, Indianapolis.

What Islam is all About. By Yahiya Emerick. Noorart
Publications, Richardson, 2002

# Video

Muhammad: Legacy of a Prophet

Inside Islam: Presented by the History Channel

A Visit to a Mosque in America: Understanding Islam and the American Muslim Community

Muslims in America: The Misunderstood Millions - ABC Nightline

Born in the USA: Muslim Americans

Inside Mecca: Presented by National Geographic

Islam: Empire of Faith: PBS Home Video

Islam and Democracy: Is a Clash of Civilizations Inevitable?

Islam in America after September 11th

Islam: A Closer Look

# Internet Resources

http://www.ifna.net

http://www.islam.com

www.islamicity.com

www.discoverislam.com

www.islamfortoday.com

http://www.islam-guide.com

http://www.jannah.org

http://www.noorart.com

http://islamicbookstore.com

http://www.cair-net.org

http://www.studyislam.com

http://www.icna.com

http://www.prophetmuhammed.org